FARAWAY

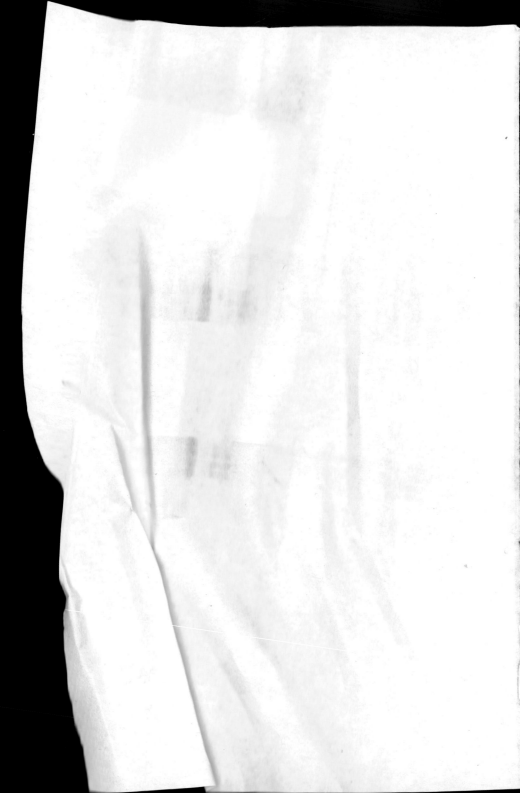

*A Suburban Boy's Story
as a Victim of Sex Trafficking*

FARAWAY

R. K. KLINE *and* **DANIEL D. MAURER**

Afterword by Dr. Richard Curtis & Dr. Anthony Marcus

Two Harbors Press
322 First Avenue N, 5th floor
Minneapolis, MN 55401
612.455.2293
www.TwoHarborsPress.com

ISBN-13: 978-1-63413-207-7
LCCN: 2014922024

Distributed by Itasca Books

Cover Design by Alan Pranke
Typeset by James Arneson

Printed in the United States of America

CONTENTS

Acknowledgments

I would like to take this opportunity to thank the people who were important in helping me to get to the place where I am today.

First, to Dan, who was one of the first to help me realize that mine was a story that people needed to hear. Without his writing skills this book wouldn't have been possible. To Dr. Gwen Sayler, who invited me to speak to the students and faculty of Wartburg Theological Seminary. This experience conveyed a feeling of honor and self-worth I'd never felt before.

To our editor Rebecca Ninke: I couldn't think of a better person to edit our work, especially one who is nearly as salty as I am. I would also like to thank my psychiatrist, Lyle Herman, who helped me walk to places I never thought I'd have the courage to go.

To Pastor Anita Hill, who will always be not just a hero, but also a champion to countless LGBTQ leaders in the ELCA. To Tim Feiertag, who has been a hero of mine from way back. He was on the front lines early on in the struggle for LGBTQ rights in the Evangelical Lutheran Church in America, and a dear friend of mine.

I also want to thank my kid, Scotty G. I could not have asked God to give me a better son than you. Our wounds come from different sources, but we've done well. I love you, kiddo. Also, thanks go to God, who was there for me in the darkest places. Finally, thanks to Stevie and Squirrel. I want the world to know you as I did. Stevie, you were my protector. Squirrel, you were—and will always be—my love.

PAX DOMINI
R. K. Kline
Kaneohe, Hawaii—August 2014

Foreword

By Daniel D. Maurer

When I first met Kevin at Wartburg Theological Seminary in 1994, I was impressed. What I mean is that he seemed like a cool guy who had it together. He could play a mean guitar, and we spent many evenings around a campfire with other guys in our class, singing Neil Young songs and delving deep into theological meanderings we pondered after having been in class together. For three years, I didn't know he was gay.

At that point in my life, I was still undecided on the "issue" of homosexuality. I had grown up a straight man in the suburbs of Minneapolis with a good family. I was raised Methodist, but through marriage had become a devoted ELCA Lutheran–so much so that I decided to pursue theology in my graduate studies. After I had finished my undergraduate studies, I eventually applied for graduate school at Wartburg Theological Seminary in Dubuque, Iowa, where Kevin and I met. It's not that I didn't have any sense that there were gay people out there. It's just that I didn't see being gay as an issue of self-identity. Like many who don't have experience personally knowing an out gay person, I was blind to the fact that sexual orientation doesn't have anything to do with choice, but the way a person feels, deep inside. It's the way he or she is born.

Kevin and I continued our friendship in school, but he never came out to me, probably because he didn't feel safe revealing that side of himself to me. However, the education at Wartburg encouraged my searching. It helped, also, that LGBTQ justice had by that time become a topic of discussion. I looked at accepting people where they were at instead of trying to take biblical quotes as barbs to push them away. I looked also to the actions of Jesus. He was a person who always identified with the outcast, the forsaken. I finally came around.

I had finished a January interim study of the Reconciling in Christ movement within the church. The organization's mission was the full participation of both laity and clergy who identified as LGBTQ. When I returned to graduate school, I felt refreshed and renewed, as if a great weight had been lifted. I no longer had to be a judge; that title belonged to someone greater than any of us. I also no longer saw same-sex attraction as an aberration or something that society needed to fix. I was an ally and I was happy to be one. I changed.

But being an ally in theory is different than being one in practice. I remember Kevin and I were sitting in a darkened Dubuque bar with some other guys in our class, drinking beer. There was a band up on the stage and the music was loud. I mentioned to Kevin that I thought the chick singing was hot (I was married at the time, but I still liked to look!).

Kevin looked directly at me and said, "Hey, Dan ... you know I'm gay?"

I was floored. No. I hadn't known that. Not at all.

I guess Kevin's coming out to me was a new link in the bonds of our friendship. That he would trust me enough to tell me who he was meant that I was on a more level playing field with our friendship.

We graduated from seminary and we each went to our respective first calls in serving as ordained pastors of the ELCA. Kevin went to Kansas. I went to western North Dakota. But we managed to keep in touch, and a few of us even got together several times in the next decade. In the meantime, I would fall hard in my addiction to alcohol and drugs. I suppose it was my own demon to bear. I struggled with depression and I didn't want to be a pastor anymore. Through it all, Kevin was one friend who stuck with me. He encouraged me to seek treatment and gave me the tough love that I needed as a friend. After going through three treatments, I finally got sober in early 2011 at the Hazelden treatment center in Center City, Minnesota. Afterward, I moved to Saint Paul, Minnesota, with my wife and two boys.

By that time, Kevin had moved on from Kansas to Hawaii. (The lucky bastard.) We managed to call each other from time to time, but distance strained our relationship. One day when I was mowing the lawn, Kevin called me up and we chatted for a while, just catching up with news between us. He told me that he had been seeing a therapist and that he had been keeping a journal. He wanted me to read it. By this time, I had become a professional freelance writer and the thought of reading something as personal as a journal piqued my interest. Before we hung up, he told me that he would send the journal via e-mail. He told me to keep it to myself. And then he told me something that I wouldn't forget, something that would remind me why we eventually came to write his story in a book: "You're never going to think of me in the same way."

Dismissing any thoughts that he had secretly killed someone or served as a CIA spy, I read his journal entries. In them, he recounted his experiences in the summer of 1975, how he was an underage male park hustler, and the story of his fellow hustlers Squirrel and Stevie. It was stunning, no doubt. But what Kevin didn't realize was that I didn't recoil out of horror or disgust. No. Instead, I was proud of him. It takes a lot to dig up your past. Then there was his relationship with Squirrel and Stevie. It was an angle I hadn't known before. The depth of their relationship was more than only a passing connection. They shared a deep bond, which, considering their circumstances, was unique and precious. I suggested that we publish his stories as a memoir. He immediately dismissed it.

Then, Gwen Sayler, a professor at Wartburg Theological Seminary, suggested that Kevin give a talk at WTS on the subject of human trafficking. He accepted and it was a resounding hit. Students and professors filled the hall, and Kevin found there were others who wanted to know his story and how it related to the problem of trafficking human beings for sex. Dr. Sayler reiterated my suggestion that Kevin should publish his story. Also around that same time, Kevin established a connection with Drs. Ric Curtis and Anthony Marcus of the John Jay College of Criminal Justice in New York City; they also encouraged him to share his story.

Since then, Kevin has worked closely with me, as well as our editor, Rebecca Ninke, who has been invaluable in refining the story for readability.

It's my hope that this book can not only be a wonderful story about the bond Kevin shared with Stevie and Squirrel, as well as a sobering meditation on the problem of sex trafficking, but that you also might see a story of hope—a theological statement proclaiming hope in the midst of tragedy and loss. Of particular interest to me is that readers know that sex trafficking not only affects girls and women, but also boys and men. In fact, the study Drs. Curtis and Marcus undertook reveals the hard fact that a large percentage of youth caught in trafficking are in fact boys. No other resource lets the public know about this fact. Kevin's story, it seems, has played out again and again for boys through the years. It's time that our ignorance of the problem ends. It's time to tell Kevin's story.

I encourage you to share this book with your friends and family, so that other boys need not suffer.

R.K. Kline, 1975.

The Gun

When I was sixteen years old, I thought I figured out how to solve all my problems.

All I needed was a gun.

Getting it was the issue. Even in the 1970s, the logistics of acquiring a gun were a challenge for a minor. My family didn't have guns in our house in Florissant, Missouri. Besides, a sixteen-year-old suburban boy couldn't just waltz into the neighborhood gun store and buy one. So I devised a plan.

My dad didn't need much convincing to take me to the Hawken Shop in suburban St. Louis. The place sold antique, replica, and collector guns. It was the sort of store Davy Crockett could have walked into, fully dressed in his mountain man costume, and no one would have batted an eye. I was a bit of history buff, and since I knew my dad was too, I thought he would have less suspicion of my real motives—I told my old man I wanted a black powder cap-and-ball pistol. This made sense to him; it probably even seemed masculine in his eyes. I thought I was brilliant; I was proud for managing to get the gun with parental approval. What I didn't consider was how it would make my dad feel to have bought the gun that his son used to shoot himself.

The gun was a replica of an 1860-something, Navy Colt .44 revolver with blued steel and a walnut pistol grip. I remember going home with it, holding it in my hands as I sat on the bed in my room. It felt heavy and powerful. Feeling the steel and the wood, smelling the gunpowder, I realized that it had the power to change a life in a second. Or end it. I wanted to change my life and end it, to stop the ache—forever. I wanted to kill myself with that gun.

But I couldn't do it.

It's not that I was chicken. Anyone who has considered suicide understands the appeal: no more never-ending hurt, no more shame, no more intrusive memories of evil faces and sad places. Living with the pain takes more guts than pulling the trigger. God knows I would have liked to have ended the suffering.

But something held me back. I wasn't sure why then. Or now.

Instead of the gun, I numbed up with alcohol, black beauties, weed, and anything I could get my hands on. But the numbness was always temporary. Morning would come. And with the breaking light, as I'd lay on my bed with my eyes open, it would all come rushing back. The images in my head seemed to taunt me. I thought I'd never be free from them. I thought I'd never be the same as I was before the summer of 1975.

One night in the fall of '77, I revisited my indecision. Nursing my new resolution with booze, I returned to my plan to stop the pain—it was time to check out. From a box in the bottom of my closet, I dug out the antique gun.

I drunkenly stumbled back to my bed and loaded up the gun, pouring in the gunpowder down the cold barrel. I remember the earthy, dank smell of the gunpowder. I remember the oily feel of the metal barrel of the gun. I took the ramrod, the thin metal rod used to load the gun, and stuffed the wad and the bullet in tight. I put the cold steel barrel in my mouth. *It's now or never, Kev.* I pulled the trigger.

CLICK!

There, in the darkness of my bedroom, I mumbled a torrent of profanities to myself. And I realized what I had just done.

It turned out I was so drunk that I had neglected to place a percussion cap on the firing mechanism ... meaning the gunpowder didn't ignite, and the bullet didn't fire. Those ball-and-cap replicas take concentration to load correctly. Had I owned a modern revolver that required a simple bullet in the chamber, I would be dead. The nerdy appeal of the complex gun ended up saving my life. That, and the fact that I was drunk. The empty *click* of that hammer falling, echoing in my mouth, brought me to the sobering realization that I had almost died. I put the gun and the suicidal thoughts away.

I'm still here.

Nearly forty years later, in 2014, the pain remains, but so does my desire to live. And now, my hope is to finally lessen the pain by telling my story. I wonder if telling my story to others will spread the pain thin? Will your awareness of my burden help carry what has weighed on me for decades?

Maybe. Deep within me, there is a need to speak of what happened years ago. I am encouraged by the goodness of new people in my life who remind me that I am more than the broken kid who tried killing himself when he was sixteen.

Looking back, I know that my existence has been defined most of all by those events of my fourteenth summer. I divide my life into two: the periods of time before and after those summer months of '75.

I didn't intend for it to be this way. But I understand now that the Kevin before 1975 doesn't exist within me anymore. Sometimes it feels like he's out living a normal life in a parallel universe. He's got his own normal story.

But I'm left with mine.

The pain that I've lived with sticks in my head and goes round and round, like a record playing a song I just don't want to hear anymore. The memories are from years ago, but they are always near, always present. Sometimes I wonder how long I can endure reliving them.

But there is something that helps sustain me. It's a painting I see every morning when I wake up and every evening as I shut off the lights. It's a copy of a painting, really. I bought it at a yard sale in Florissant before I went to grad school. I'd seen it long ago, in either a museum or an art history book. It's an Andrew Wyeth painting of a little blond kid, sitting in a field of brown grass. He's hugging his knees close to his chest. He wears a coonskin cap like Davy Crockett and has on a black jacket and blue jeans. What strikes me about this painting is the boy's face, especially his eyes. He's looking off in the distance, but it's sort of down and away, like he's looking at me, but he's not looking at me either. It's like the boy is looking *through* me. It's like his soul is lost and his mind is far from him. Which is perhaps the reason Mr. Wyeth named the painting *Faraway*.

What I feel most of all about this painting is that I know that boy. I met him in the summer of 1975. To me, he is both far away and always near. He lives in my pain and is still never near enough.

I have wondered: If the pain will go away, will I lose the memories of the boy too?

What would be left?

FARAWAY, 1952 drybrush © Andrew Wyeth. Reprinted with permission.

Being Gay

Years before the summer of '75, when I first started breaking into puberty, I began meeting other boys my age who were also dealing with same-sex attraction. Jeff, Nelson, Damon: those are just a few names I remember. I figured out quickly I was gay and I was just fine with it. As fourteen-year-old boys, we were full of hormones and had easy access to each other. In fact, we had more opportunity to experiment than straight kids. You see, if you're a fourteen-year-old straight boy asking your parents if your cute friend Sally can spend the night with you outside in a pup tent, Mom and Dad will naturally say: *"Hell no!"*

Compare that with: "Hey, Mom, can my friend Jeff spend the night?"

"Why, sure Kevin, that'd be lovely."

"Mom, can we set up the camping tent outside and sleep out there?"

"Well, sure. But your bed's plenty big for the two of you; why don't you boys just sleep there?"

"Thanks, Mom. You're the best!"

Get my drift?

Especially in the 1970s and even now, many people assume that boys are straight by nature. But that's not the way it works all the time; at least that's not the way it was with me. I'd figured out quickly I was gay and I was OK with it. One time when I was twelve, my friend Damon and I were outside in the backyard. It was summer and hot. We were in our bathing suits, playing in our aboveground pool. I remember looking at him while he played there in his bathing suit and feeling attracted to him. I'd never experienced anything like that with a girl. It clicked then (and from then on) that I was attracted to people of the same gender. For me, it was just attraction.

Don't get the wrong idea. At our age, it's not like we were engaging in wild, uncontrollable sex. We were innocent fourteen-year-old boys. What we did was sexual, but it was quite harmless, certainly inexperienced, and–when I'm honest and bold about claiming my sexuality–normal.

In 1975, there were no role models for us. Given society's views about homosexuality, we were completely on our own, trying to find our way the best we could. There was no observing others to learn how we were supposed to act. There were no shows on television portraying a healthy gay family. There were no dances for us, no talks about rules for dating. We were left to fend for ourselves in the wilderness. Like anyone else growing up, we had to watch for dangers and predators. But in our case, there was no one to protect us. The danger was real. I cannot express strongly enough how everyone who was gay lived with the constant threat of violence or rejection.

I remember one time in particular, when I was twelve. We were all sitting in the living room watching the evening news. Normally, I didn't pay much attention to the news. Yet that night one report grabbed me by my shirt and glued my eyes to the TV. A fire had occurred at a New Orleans bar called the Upstairs Lounge, killing thirty-two patrons. The reporter said it was arson. As we watched, the report showed scenes of the near-total destruction of the building. I remember the reporter saying that the bar was a frequent hangout for homosexuals, and that many of the bodies couldn't be claimed since most or all of the men had been carrying fake IDs. Some claimed the fire was intentional. I didn't doubt that at all. Since then, I've come to understand that this event was probably the largest gay murder in US history, certainly within New Orleans's history.

When the report was over, everyone in my family–my folks and my brother and my sister–just sat there. It's not like my dad or my mom would have commented anyway–they weren't the type to give a running appraisal about politics or current events. But their silence after the report made me feel that they were giving an implied disapproval for the guys in the fire. It was like: Yes, the fire happened. People died. That's sad. But they shouldn't have been there in the first place.

You need to understand that my parents were rarely vocal about their disapproval of gays. To me, it was more the "accepted understanding" everyone in society, including my family, had about gays. Because of that understanding, I understood where I belonged: in the closet. To do anything else would be to invite not only their disapproval, but (I feared) their implicit rejection of me. There's another time that comes to mind. One day, my sister and I were riding our school bus home. She was a sophomore in high school and I was in seventh grade, but our schools were right next to each other in Florissant, so we both rode the same bus. Riding on the same bus with us was an overweight, effeminate kid whom the bullies liked to pick on, who got off at the stop before ours. Up to that point, the teasing had only been verbal. That day, however, a bunch of guys got off at that kid's stop, which wasn't where they would have normally gotten off. Right before the driver closed the door and headed toward our house, my sister stomped up the center aisle from where she'd been sitting behind me. She grabbed the collar of my jean jacket and pulled me out of my seat.

I said to her, "What? This isn't our stop." She didn't reply, but only looked me in the eyes with furled eyebrows and her lips pinched together in a little frown showing me she meant business. She pushed me from behind and I stumbled forward.

As we bounded down the bus stairs and stepped outside, I saw the little kid ahead of us and the boys following close behind. My sister and I were farther back. The school bus door closed with a click and the diesel engine revved up as the bus pulled away. I saw the boys rush after the effeminate boy and heard him squeal one single word: "No!"

And then we watched the other boys beat the living snot out of him.

"Should we help him?" I asked, knowing the answer.

"Shut up," was all she replied.

The boy screamed. He cried. I can hear his screams and cries to this day.

I never knew the reason why my sister made me get off the bus that day. I've thought about this recently, and I think that maybe she was only curious to see what would happen to him. Maybe she just wanted to see a fight. The way I took it then, however, was that she was giving her younger brother a message, a lesson he shouldn't forget: this is what happens to little fags—you'd better watch out. Maybe she thought that what would happen to that poor kid, how he would inevitably scream and cry, would end up leaving a bigger impression on me than simply telling me to stop being a sissy. There's no doubt it left a negative impression on me. And fear. I guess my sister got what she wanted.

Among my own group of gay friends, none of us appeared effeminate. We hid our gayness well, considering what could happen to us if we were found out. I don't think we acted differently than the straight boys—we were just an average bunch of rough-and-tumble guys. I could be wrong though; after all, we were able to find each other. It was the magic of "gaydar," I suppose. Intuitively knowing who's gay doesn't come down to whether a person's sexuality is accepted in society.

My friendships differed from those of most of my school friends in one respect: usually after a friend spent the night, I wouldn't hear from him again. The lasting connections I sought were in conflict with the horrible self-loathing and fear that our society burdened us with. This stigma is evolving for the better I believe, but back then, that's the way it was. I would have welcomed a friend who was like me, who knew who I was and accepted it.

My friendships during those years weren't just about our sexuality. A fear I have about recounting this story today is that people will read it and focus on the sex. *This is not a story about sex.* This is a story about friendship and faith, love and survival. It is set in the tragic context of an account of sex trafficking, perhaps in a world you weren't aware of. Although the way sex trafficking plays out today is different than how it played out back then, some things never change—people still use other people, kids even.

This tragedy unfolds in a new way in every generation. Thousands, if not tens of thousands or hundreds of thousands, have fallen prey to human trafficking. The problem is bigger than what happened to me. However, mine is a story not often told because it is doubly taboo: I was a child prostitute and I was gay. The public focus of prostitution predominantly addresses the involvement of girls and young women, but there are other voices to be heard.

This story is *my* story. And I'm going to tell it like it was.

Ray

When I was fourteen, my friend Tim came over, saying he had something to tell me. I'd met Tim at Hazelwood Junior High, where he was assigned the seat in front of me in our remedial eighth-grade English class, toward the back of the room. Tim and I quickly became aware that our sexuality was on the same plane. Kids like us always seemed to find each other. It must have been that gay intuition at work.

Whenever we were off by ourselves, Tim had a tendency to always bring the conversation back to oral sex. Of course, those conversations got us both interested. And that led to get-togethers after school.

When I think of it now, what strikes me most about Tim is that when it came to the actual sexual act, he was an intermediary between my earlier partners and my first experience with an adult. Pretty much all of the sex we had was opportunistic, occurring whenever we could manage to be alone. We never really fully disrobed, but managed sex with our pants down around our ankles. In this manner it wasn't unlike my earlier sexual encounters. With the boys before, sex usually consisted of hand jobs, followed by a blow job. Once or twice we embraced and I remember one sloppy, amateur kiss.

Tim would do all this as well, but man, it was the oral sex he took to a new level. One time we found thirty minutes to ourselves in his dad's garage. He pushed me and held me up against the garage wall. He lifted up my shirt, working on my chest and stomach with his lips as he made his way down. Once there, he wouldn't just go up and down, but upside, downside, underneath, and all around.

The first time, I was literally speechless. When I finally found the words to describe what had just happened, the only thing I could manage to say was: "Whoa! Where'd you learn all that?!"

"A friend. I'll let you meet him sometime." This statement piqued my interest. *Who, I wonder?*

When it was my turn to reciprocate, Tim's gentle moaning built to a peak, so I must have done all right. I'd clearly been eager to learn.

When we were done, I was anxious to get home, but even more interested to meet who had taught Tim his magical sex tricks.

"Um … Tim?" I said.

"Yeah?"

"You said that some guys taught you how to do all that great stuff. Who? Do they go to our school?"

"No. Man, these guys are older," Tim said, shaking his head and smiling.

"What, like … *adults*?"

"Yeah. I'll introduce you to one of 'em. His name is Ray."

Ray, I thought. *I bet he's pretty cool.*

Looking back on your life, there are some moments where you wish you could tell your younger self: *Go in the opposite direction. Run.*

But I didn't. Why? Because I was interested.

I got on my bike and headed back to my house, back to my other life in suburbia.

TO UNDERSTAND my story, you need to know a little Midwest geography: Florissant, Missouri, is one of several small towns in St. Louis County, a large area that surrounds all of the city of St. Louis. St. Louis is an independent city, meaning its city government has chosen to be separate from the larger county.

Now imagine a donut. The part that's the left-hand side is St. Louis County, and the donut hole is the city. Now cut the donut in half. The Mississippi River represents the cut, as well as the border with the state of Illinois.

If you ask a St. Louis County native where he hails from, he'll just say: "St. Louis," regardless of whether he grew up in St. Louis County or St. Louis the city. If you're also from St. Louis, the conversation will invariably get around to where you both went to high school. This accomplishes two things: first, it says where in St. Louis County (or city) you grew up, and second, it establishes "which side of the tracks" you call home.

Florissant is in north St. Louis County. In the mid-1970s, it was a solidly blue-collar, working-class Roman Catholic suburb. Many of the folks who lived there worked either at the Ford plant or the McDonnell Douglas plant. My family and I moved to Florissant from Oklahoma in 1968.

I was born in St. Louis, but lived in Oklahoma as a toddler. My dad, a chiropractor, had a busy office in Bristow, a town about thirty-five miles southwest of Tulsa. Yet despite my father's success, my mother didn't want to live there. Since so much of her family of origin was from St. Louis, she wanted to get back into that area. My dad worshipped the ground my mother walked on and loved her deeply. So at my mother's request, our family ended up moving back to Missouri when I was four, to a suburb of St. Louis–Ferguson.

I went to kindergarten, and first and second grade, at Valley Winds Elementary School in Ferguson. As it happens, the school had just received an award in December of 1965, for being the "Nation's School of the Year." People knew Valley Winds as the "progressive" school in the St. Louis area.

Ferguson at that time was a run-of-the-mill, middle-class suburb. All in all, it was a nice town. Our neighborhood was a relatively inexpensive place where young families just starting out could begin their lives. In the 1970s, however, the genetic makeup of Ferguson began to change, especially after the in-famous Pruitt-Igoe housing projects were destroyed in 1972.

Suddenly urban blacks began moving into the nearby and surrounding suburbs.

The resulting "white flight" was typical of a lot of north St. Louis County. Today the neighborhood where I lived is still a place for young families just getting started. The main difference now is that kids there don't have the opportunities I once had. For them, it's a toss-up over whether to fear criminals or the cops more. Sadly, our house was right around the corner from where Michael Brown was shot in 2014.

We ended up moving once more to Florissant when I was seven, where the story in this book takes place. Our little family was normal as normal could be. What I mean is that we weren't dysfunctional, but pretty average as families go. My mother and father loved each other very much, as well as us kids. They always got us to school, fed us, and chatted daily with us, asking all the questions parents normally ask their kids:

"How was your day today?"

"What new things are you learning in school?"

"We need to get our bags packed for our trip next week."

"Kevin!! Get out and mow the lawn! I've been telling you to mow it for two days now."

You know … normal family stuff. We were the typical suburban family just living our lives in our own version of Mayberry or Mayfield.

Other than the daily conversation that comes from living with another person, I didn't speak much with my older sister. I didn't talk much with my younger brother either, who was a year-and-a-half younger than me. Although, I have to say, we didn't always get along. Our house was small, and out of necessity, we shared a room. Maybe it was because my sister got her own room, but I grew resentful of the fact that I had to share my room with my brother. I'd fight from time to time with my brother over normal sibling things. He'd get his revenge by telling on me to our parents. Because of this, I was very protective of my personal life with my brother, and I'd never share my sexual identity with him. I eventually got my own room, but that was after the events of the summer of '75.

Our neighborhood, as well as most of the others around us, was built on farmland. In fact, the old farmhouse that used to occupy our property was still behind our place. For several years after we moved in, construction workers were building houses in and around our block.

Florissant had the usual corner bars, but the one I remember most was BJ's. It was small, always packed, and had a cork ball court in the back. My dad never went there, but it was a part of the culture of our town.

I was eleven or twelve the first time I remember getting drunk; however, it wasn't at BJ's. By thirteen I was smoking weed. For me, drinking and smoking weed were ways of trying to fit in, wanting to feel mature.

I suppose Florissant was a decent place to grow up. All of our parents smoked, and all of our parents drank to some extent, though my dad was never a heavy drinker. Sometimes your friends would show up to school with a bruise or two, but unless something was broken, no one said a thing. That's what it was like then; thankfully, my parents were pretty good on that front.

Back in my living room, Tim told me again how he knew some men who would actually give you ten, fifteen dollars if you let them give you a blow job. I remember that it took me a second or two to wrap my fourteen-year-old mind around the concept of this, but in no time, it seemed to make sense. Blow jobs were great, and having money would be nice for a change. The idea intrigued me, and I told Tim I wanted to know more.

"Yeah, Kevin, it's hot," Tim said. "The guys blow *you* and you get money!"

I was curious. "Where ... uh, you know, do you go, to ... uh, you know ... to do it?"

"Oh, there's this park in the city," Tim said. "Sometimes it's in cars. Hey, do you want to go with me this next week?"

I tried not to act too interested, but I got Tim to agree to take me with him on his next adventure. I didn't need much convincing. I wanted to know more.

He told me about going to St. Ferdinand Park, a local suburban park just around the corner from where I lived. It wasn't a large park, but it was packed with ball fields. "Well, you know," Tim said, "you can come with and all ... but I hope you're not too dumb. I'm just saying–don't be a dork. OK?"

This puzzled me. "What do you mean?"

He didn't seem to want to explain. "Don't worry about it. Just come with me next week. I'll let you meet Ray. He's pretty cool."

I'd be lying if I told you the time waiting for it all to happen was easy to bear. It wasn't. I was curious. I was interested. And, I guess I was excited. I thought it would be a summer adventure–a kind of fantasy quest–where I could be myself and make a few bucks. Little did I know how foolish and naive this attitude would turn out for me.

That next week, just as school was about to let out and all the possibilities for a fourteen-year-old standing at the threshold of summer seemed endless, we hiked to St. Ferdinand Park to hang out and watch the many ball games that were always going on. It was a late Saturday night in May.

Before '75, I always enjoyed going to the park. I'd especially like the times when nobody was around, which was often in the late evening hours. I'd go there all by myself and just allow myself the time to be alone. I felt safe going there, not only because it was so close to my house, but also because it was my special place, and I could simply dream or dwell in my own thoughts. That summer would change what the park meant for me. No doubt, that summer changed a lot of places, and what they can mean for me.

As we walked to the park from my neighborhood, we crossed a bridge going over Coldwater Creek. We got on a dirt path and passed through the open fields to get to the baseball diamonds. In the distance beyond the ball fields was a beautiful recreational pond. Since that night I've learned that the park used to be an old fruit orchard, and that three German children are buried there–another tragic story. The graves are still right there in the park, in the center of a circle of cedar trees. Perhaps the dead could have warned me about what was going to happen to me. However, that evening I noticed no signs or omens of the danger ahead.

AS TIM AND I walked through the park, I was a ball of nerves. When I was scared, I got quiet. Tim must have noticed this earlier, as he mentioned how quiet I was while we were walking to the park. He'd said, "Don't worry, man, this guy is really nice." Apparently it had all been an arranged date.

Tim and I went over to a game where some other kids were playing. We sat on the bleachers at the ball diamond that was closest to the park pond and the restrooms. In no time, a thirtysomething man arrived and sat down next to Tim. Tim quickly introduced me to him.

"Kevin," Tim said, "this is Ray."

"Hi," I said, looking at Ray. I smiled and tried to look tough, maybe a little more grown up.

Ray looked into my eyes and said, "Hello, Kevin." He smiled widely–not just with his lips, but with his eyes too. This was no fake smile.

An uncomfortable pause hung in the air. We sat down next to each other in the bleachers. It was far enough away from the other people watching the game so that they couldn't hear us. I sat next to Ray.

He continued, "You like baseball, Kevin?"

"Yeah. Well … no. I mean … I don't like to play it, but I like to watch. I like the Cardinals."

"Gotta root for the home team, man. Right on." Ray reached down into a clear plastic bag. It crinkled as he pulled out a handful of peanuts in the shell. "Want some?" he asked me, holding up the bag.

"Nah."

"Come on, they're good."

"OK." I grabbed a few peanuts.

"So you don't play baseball. How about any other sports?"

"Nah. Not really."

"Really? You don't throw a football around once in a while with your ol' man or your brother?"

"Well. I s'pose that. But, not really."

"OK. That's cool. What do you like to do, Kevin?"

"I dunno. I like to make models."

"Models?"

"Yeah. Like model airplanes and ships. Maybe some cars." There was one model I was especially proud of. "I built a model of the Arizona … you know, the battleship. It was the one that sunk in Pearl Harbor."

"Oh yeah?! That's cool! I like how you can set them all up afterwards and just stare at them. It's like you can imagine yourself flying that plane in World War II. That you're the one shooting down all the Nazis." Ray held up his hands as if to hold a gun and shook them back and forth, imitating the recoil from an automatic weapon. He made crashing explosion noises showing me that he shot down an enemy plane. He smiled again.

As Ray talked, I thought to myself, *Wow, he really is a nice guy, and he looks really cool!* (Saying that a guy was *really cool* was my way of saying that he was good-looking.) Obviously, Ray knew how to talk with kids. He had an air of playfulness to him that didn't match his age. It put me at ease.

Suddenly, Tim got up to leave. The game we were watching was long from finishing.

"Hey Kev … I gotta go clean up my room or my mom's gonna kill me. I'll meet you later. Go ahead and hang with Ray for a bit."

And before I knew it, Tim got up and left. "Seeya!" he said.

For some reason, I stayed.

Ray never struck me as *creepy*. Not at all. I warmed to him gradually because he was nice. He was relaxed when he spoke, entering as he did into my nerdy world of model cars and planes and boats. I'd quickly learn that Ray had the gift of skillfully blending into whatever situation he found himself in. He was like a chameleon.

Ray and I continued to talk, which was fine, but the longer we talked, the more anxious I got. I wasn't doing anything that would have stuck out to others, but I understood I was sitting with and talking to an adult who wanted to have sex with me. What was making me nervous was the fear that someone I knew was going to see me and ask questions. My eyes flicked back and forth, scanning the bleachers and looking at people coming into the park, but I never saw anyone I recognized.

Ray continued talking and asking me questions. It never seemed like he was grilling me, just that he wanted to chat, like I was his bud. It made me feel grown up, like I was going on a date.

"You ever been to Ted Drewes?" Ray asked.

"No. Who's he?" I didn't know who that was, or where Ted lived.

Ray chuckled. "Hehe. No. Not *a guy* … well, he was a real guy. But I was talking about the place you get ice cream in the city. Ted Drewes is the shop."

My face got red. "Oh. No."

"Oh, and it's not ice cream. It's *frozen custard*."

"Really?"

"Oh, man. It's the best! Like you're eating pure cream of all creams with whatever flavor you want. It's awesome. You should check it out. Maybe I'll bring you there. Would you like that?"

"Sure. Yeah!"

Another uncomfortable pause hung in the air. It was like watching a ball game on TV, when the producers zeroed in on a home run ball hanging in the air, filming it in slow motion. Except, for me, the anticipation was almost unbearable. I liked Ray. I was excited. I wanted to know where all of our conversation was leading. But Ray didn't look anxious or uncomfortable in the least, a fact that made it more unbearable for me. He was just so … *cool*.

I mentioned that I'd been to another ice cream shop: "I've been to the St. Charles Dairy. Ever been there?"

"Yeah! That's the place that has those great chocolate sodas, right?"

"Yeah!" I said. I was enjoying talking with him, but another side of me was itching.

Apparently, Ray could see this. "Wanna go check out my van?" he asked. "It's decked out."

Ray stood up first. I followed. My heart was about to explode out of my chest. As we politely excused ourselves to get around the other spectators in the bleachers, I thought to myself that I had something here. I had a love, I thought. Everyone else was focused on the stupid game. Not me. We were going to hang out, together. In a van. *Ray's van*.

The parking lot sat directly next to the fields, so we didn't have to walk far. Still, his van seemed so distant. That's how dilated time seemed to me. Seconds were thick, like honey, full of anticipation.

Ray owned one of those groovy mid-seventies-style vans. It was sky blue and silver and had little bubbly windows in the back. The design made it look like a spaceship, I thought. As I opened the passenger door and climbed in, I entered a whole new world. I'd never seen a van like Ray's before, not the inside of one, at least. I looked to the back, past a couple of dark velvet curtains. There was a twin bed off to one side with off-white cotton sheets. A folded purple blanket lay in the corner, stuffed between the mattress and the wall of the van. On both sides of the bed I saw what looked like small shelves built into the walls. There were several things strewn about: clothes, a baseball glove, and a couple of soccer balls near the back. On the shelves were four or five 8-track tapes, all haphazardly stacked. The item that grabbed my attention was a jar of Vaseline. I may have been fourteen, but I immediately knew what that was for.

After glancing around and taking inventory, I took a quick, deep breath and wiggled to the rear of the vehicle, where I sat on the bed. Ray must have seen that the Vaseline caught my attention. "Do you want me to use some of that tonight?" he asked.

"What, you mean … like … butt sex?"

"Yeah, butt sex. Ah … maybe next time," he said. "Come back on up front. Sit down. I'm gonna take us someplace nice." I shimmied back to the passenger seat and sat down. Ray fired up the engine.

"Where we goin'?" I asked.

"Ah … just somewhere where nobody'll see us. It's not far," he said.

We drove away from the bleachers and left the entrance of St. Ferdinand Park. Ray turned right down Lindbergh Boulevard until we got to Charbonier Road and took another right. We traveled about a mile and then continued all the way down until we came to what the locals called "Mo Bottoms." It was always pitch black down there and out in the "country," though it was only one mile down the road. Ray pulled the van off onto a secluded side road, parked, and turned off the engine. For about ten seconds, we sat in silence. Ray spoke first.

"So here we are. What d'ya wanna do?"

"I don't know … suck, I guess."

It must have been obvious I was relatively new to it all, at least with an adult.

"Well come on then," he said.

Ray went to the back of the van and began to undress on top of the mattress. He was suddenly completely naked, sitting there on the mattress. I guess I didn't know what to expect, but it wasn't a naked guy right there in front of me all of a sudden.

"Well, are you going to take your clothes off, or what?"

So that's what I did.

When we first met, I thought Ray was very hot. He had big brown eyes, and very, very dark brown hair–almost black. It was shoulder length and feathered. He wore a cool mustache, and it looked natural on him. Nothing cheesy. His style was very hip for the seventies. He was also well built; he had a well-defined chest and shoulder muscles, and just the right amount of hair on his chest.

By the time I'd taken off my boondockers, pants, and shirt, it must have been obvious to Ray how excited I was.

"Lie down," he said. He lay on top of me. I could tell he was trying to not let his weight bear down on me too much. But then he let more of his muscled bulk down and our bodies were on top of each other. With all of him on top of me, I let out a high-pitched moan, a squeak even. That made him laugh. "I got you now, kid," he said. We giggled for a bit after this, joking together.

As we embraced, he tried to kiss me, but each time I'd turn my head away. I think I did this mainly because I simply didn't know how. Ray didn't seem to care about that, and went on doing what he was doing ... and I liked what he was doing. Before I knew it, it was over. We were done.

WE WEREN'T gone for more than an hour and a half.

After we had sex, Ray gave me his number and twenty bucks. He then drove me home, dropped me off two blocks before my house, and smiled at me–a big, fake Cheshire-cat smile. "Hey, see ya, Kev," he said.

"Yeah," I said. I waited awhile, just looking back at him. Then, I said something that surprised me. "Do you wanna meet again?" I wasn't usually that forward. At least, I surprised myself because the words sort of just came out.

"Sure. I'd really like to be with you again. Me and you. That's what it's all about, right?"

Wow, I thought. *Me and you, he said. Me and Ray!* I'd be lying if I said I wasn't excited. That's the thing–I never felt "used" in any way by Ray during our first encounter. It was ... so natural. That's what I thought. There was an unsettled feeling in me, though. Like I was getting away with something. It's the feeling you get when you know what you're doing is wrong, but do it anyway. It's exciting to break the rules.

I walked home feeling confused, yet grown up. Mature. Wanted. The excitement about the whole affair was real, but it wasn't like I thought it would be. Later, I'd read that female prostitutes often feel dirty after doing the act for the first time. It wasn't like that for me. I just didn't know what it meant. Certainly I didn't think of myself as a whore. Not then. The fact that Ray had given me twenty dollars scared the hell out of me, though, and not because it made me a child prostitute. Instead, it was the *amount* of money that made me feel uncomfortable. Twenty bucks was a lot of money in '75. How the hell was a suburban kid going to explain having wads of cash in his possession? I remember every detail walking home, how the trees looked so crisp in the spring. How warm I felt inside.

It's funny, isn't it? How we remember all the details about our firsts?

Looking back, I had no idea what was going on, even though I thought I did. I hadn't connected the dots. Not yet. I didn't consider what Ray had done as anything else than him just being nice to me. My plan for the summer to find a boyfriend, have a little fun, and make a few bucks was sharply divorced from the reality of the situation. Ray, of course, had a different plan.

After that night, I never spoke with my buddy Tim again during the summer. It turned out he was essentially delivering me to Ray to be trained. I'll reiterate: everything took place right in the middle of suburban north St. Louis County, and as far as I know, no one even suspected what was going on.

I guess we all looked too normal.

The Delivery

Ray and I hooked up together a few more times after that first day. He taught me some new things, and I got to explore my sexuality more. I felt like I was falling for him. What I didn't realize is that my perspective of the relationship was on one side of the coin, while Ray's was on the other. It strikes me that I never caught on that he was using me, training me up *to be used* by him. I was a kid, after all. But when I think back now on my state of mind at the time, I don't believe I was particularly gullible or stupid. Or maybe it was just a clue as to how good Ray was at manipulating kids.

Back then, we boys had a lot more freedom to roam. It wasn't that our parents didn't care about us or what we were doing. Kids just got out and did stuff on their own. Of course, that meant that I took advantage of my folks' attitude. You need to know that this wasn't uncommon or somehow lenient. It certainly didn't mean they didn't care. It just meant that, like most kids my age, I wanted to be mature and independent. I was no different than others, and I'd try to get away with whatever I could. I remember a certain exchange in particular.

One evening, when the summer sun began to set, my mom was working in the kitchen washing dishes in the sink. She'd recently come home from her job at Smith-Scharff, a paper products company, where she ran the company's huge, ancient computers. During the day my sister watched us, but the real gatekeepers were my parents: if I wanted to get out, I'd have to secure permission from them.

It was hot, and the water in the sink made the room humid. Despite this, my mother didn't sweat, since our house had one amenity that most didn't in our neighborhood–central air. I cannot stress enough what a luxury this was in a Missouri summer (even early summer), largely because of the amount of time I spent outside, but also because some of the homes I stayed at didn't have air conditioning. Our family had it good.

I had been watching TV with my brother and my dad when my mom called me from the kitchen.

"Kevvy. Come in here. I want to talk with you."

I got up from lying on the floor and went to the kitchen. "Yeah?" I asked.

"Honey, your father and I want to play cards on Saturday at Pete and Dot's. What do you have planned?"

"Oh. Uh … I'm gonna spend the night at a friend's house." I did this all the time; it was an easy lie.

"That sounds like fun. Who?"

"Who?"

"Yes. Whose house are you staying at?"

"Jeff's. He's from Hazelwood." I knew that saying this would work. Besides the fact that in the seventies, parents didn't normally check up on their kids like they do today, my answer secured my story doubly so, because Jeff (actually one of my friends in the normal side of my life) lived in an adjacent community. I would be far enough away that my mom would no doubt buy my story.

"Well you have a good time, dear. Oh … do you need your dad to give you a ride?"

"Nah. Jeff's dad is gonna pick me up."

My mom smiled, wiped off the final plate in the sink, and pulled the plug. The soapy water went down the drain with a slurpy sound and my mom dried her hands. She looked at me, smiled again, and scruffed my hair.

Most exchanges went this way. My parents loved and cared for me as much as any well-adjusted suburban parents would in that day—a point that made my deception all the more guilt inducing after the summer was over.

While other kids may have been digging in their garages to get their baseball gloves or riding their bikes to a friend's place, all I could think about was getting to Ray. It was going to be my special summer with my special friend. I felt grown up. Cunning and crafty. I thought I'd be getting what I wanted.

The Saturday after our first encounter, I went back to St. Ferdinand Park by myself to see Ray. I was early enough so that any ball team was hours away from gathering to practice. Ray had parked outside the fence, near to where I was sitting in the empty bleachers looking over a deserted ball field. Since the park itself is quite large and open, and the ball fields take up the most space, you get the feeling that you're exposed. This might put some people ill at ease, but it was somehow comforting for me, especially since that Saturday there was no one else around. I could see far and wide that Ray was the only one there and, at that moment at least, I wasn't afraid of him.

The Missouri summer sun hadn't settled in full force yet, but you could still see the heat rise off the pavement. Ray got out of his van and walked toward me. He didn't greet me. Instead, the first thing he said was, "Hey, Kev, I've got a good friend who'd love to meet you."

Why would a good friend of Ray's want to meet me?

Ray sensed my discomfort and easily improvised.

"He likes to do the same kind of things we do together." He paused, looked down at me, and smiled. "He'd like to get to know you. I know that."

I sat in the bleachers, wondering what to say. I said what a kid does when he wants to be liked: I asked, "Is he cool?"

"Absolutely, Kevin. You'll love him."

"Yeah, OK. I guess." I expected to be spending time with Ray, and only Ray. It was just supposed to be the two of us, a real romantic weekend. Those were my expectations anyway. Ray had made it sound like it was always going to be me and him. Just us. So at first, I didn't mind the idea of meeting a friend of his. Only, I really wanted Ray to be there.

It was still early that Saturday evening when we pulled up in front of what seemed like a mansion to me. It was a big house somewhere in south St. Louis. We stopped Ray's blue van in front, and Ray said to me, "Go on in, he's waiting for you."

My thoughts stopped. "Uh, aren't you coming with me?"

"Nah. I've got a few things to do. You go ahead. This guy's nice. You'll see. Don't worry, man!"

"But I don't know him."

"You didn't know me a couple of weeks ago, did you?"

"No. I s'pose not."

"Well, then … go use your charm. Just be nice to him. He'll be nice back. You'll see. I'll be back before you know it."

Ray smiled. I didn't smile back. Then he got scary. First, he grabbed the wheel and his knuckles went white. His nostrils flared and his lips tightened. He looked outside, through the van's windshield. I imagine that the devious gears in his head were spinning around, thinking of the best way to respond to me. It was the first time I'd seen this side of him.

"Look," he said. "You *WILL* get out of this van. You *WILL* spend time with my friend. And you *WILL* be nice to him. If you don't, Kevin, I'll know. You know I will."

Fear took ahold of me. I complied. Before I knew it, I was out of the blue van and standing in front of a strange man's house.

"Please, Ray!" I pleaded as the van drove off, spinning its tires.

I stood in front of the big house. It was decision time. When you're afraid, it often seems like going with the flow is the courageous thing to do. I didn't understand then that running as fast as I could, away from that house, would have been the real brave choice.

I walked up to the front door and rang the doorbell.

A GOOD-LOOKING guy around forty or fifty answered the door. When I say he was good-looking, I mean that he wasn't hideous or scary. I was a fourteen-year-old boy, after all. He was dressed like my dad would dress when he was trying to be easygoing on the weekend around guests—a pair of brown casual slacks, a pullover shirt, and a pair of loafers.

What happened next must have had something do with my upbringing. My dad's mother was born in the South; her sense of manners was passed down to my dad and then on to me. Anyone born in the South knows that a sense of good manners is not something bred in people, but learned. I had been taught well.

I extended my hand to shake his and said, "Hello, sir, I'm Kevin, Ray's friend."

Apparently he got a kick out of this because a big, stupid smile appeared on his face and he chuckled.

"Why hello, Kevin. You can call me Jim."

Jim undoubtedly lived in a nice house. From what I could gather, he was a family man, because I saw pictures of two boys and a girl hanging in the hallway. I noticed that his family looked similar to my own family. This simultaneously comforted me and disgusted me.

Walking deeper into his home, Jim asked me if I was hungry. I was beginning to feel a little more at ease. The surroundings were unthreatening, even downright homey and familiar. I realized that I was indeed hungry. Ray hadn't taken the time to feed me before he'd pushed me out of his van.

"Sure," I said. "Yeah. That'd be great."

Jim took me down the hall to his kitchen and opened his fridge. "How about a sandwich?"

"Sounds good."

Son of a bitch if I wasn't starting to warm up to this guy.

I was thinking he'd make me a PB and J or a baloney sandwich, but Jim started listing off all kinds of meats: "Chicken? Turkey? Roast beef? What'll it be?"

He finally said, "I don't suppose you're a Braunschweiger man?"

"I love Braunschweiger, Jim!" (I still love Braunschweiger, a type of liverwurst.)

I was actually getting kind of cheeky. So, he made me a Braunschweiger sandwich and put it on a white porcelain plate with some Charles Chips. That's right–real Charles Chips in the brown-and-gold tin can that the guy in the truck delivered directly to your home.

This guy is OK, I thought. I felt my shoulders ease down away from my neck. The lump in my throat subsided.

Jim started to pour me a glass of milk, when I stopped him. "Oh. Sorry Jim, I can't drink milk; it makes me sick."

Jim froze, puzzled.

"What'd you mean? I thought all kids like milk ..."

"I guess I'm just not a normal kid," I said, looking him dead in the eyes. This seemed to break the little game of normalcy we were trying to play. There was a brief silence, and then I said, "I'd love a Coke if you have it."

Jim paused briefly, grinned, and walked into a little pantry off the kitchen. He then set out a bottled Coke on the kitchen counter, nearly slamming it down as if to say, *"There, you happy?"* He turned around and opened the cupboard where someone–I guessed his wife–had neatly stacked glass cups with their children's names embossed on the front in big brown letters. He took out a white cup with **THOMAS** written in bold letters on the front of it, filled it with the fizzy, warm Coke, and set it in front of me.

"Drink up," he said.

I took it to be more of a command than a request.

When I finished, he said, not really asking, "You ready, Kevin?"

"I guess."

All that business with the Braunschweiger and the Charles Chips and the Coke was nice. But it was bullshit, because–let's be real–I was there for Jim to fuck me.

I was there because Jim wanted a kid to fuck. Ray had shown me just how that was done. After we played nice, Jim took me upstairs to a bedroom that was obviously one of his son's bedrooms and had sex with me on his own kid's bed. Talk about messed up.

Nothing traumatic happened. That's what I thought at the time. The sex was not unpleasant, and I mostly kept thinking, *Wow, this kid's got a nice room*. But the fact of the matter was that it was completely, totally messed up. Add to that fact that my "delivery" set me on a new path that night, one that I didn't think I could stray from.

I've always wondered if that boy found out about his old man. And I wonder how many stories are out there just like mine, stories about dads having sex with someone else's child while the wife and kids were out. I wonder how many cups are out there with **THOMAS** embossed in bold letters, cups that are neatly stacked in a cupboard … cups that dear old Dad bought for his son, only to fill them with warm Coke and give them to a kid with whom he was preparing to do … sexual things.

Once we were done, I got dressed and went downstairs with Jim to wait for Ray to show up. Ray arrived in his big blue Faggin' Wagon. (I didn't actually know at that particular time that Ray's van had that ingenious name, but I soon learned it from others who knew the truth about Ray and what that van represented.)

Just as I was fixing to bounce out the door, Jim caught my arm. "Here, give this to Ray."

He put a white envelope in my hand; it had some heft and width to it, and I realized it contained a nice quantity of cash. Now call me naive or stupid, but up to that exact moment, the idea that I was involved in prostitution never even entered my head. But as soon as Jim placed that envelope in my hand, I knew exactly why I had been there and what I had just done.

After all this, I understood why Ray had brought me there. I was fourteen, but I knew damn well what a prostitute was. *He tricked me!* Any naïveté I previously had about my relationship with Ray was gone. I was no salty street kid by any stretch of the imagination. I was a cute little fourteen-year-old gay nerd from the suburbs who read *The Chronicles of Narnia* and *The Lord of the Rings*. Despite my youth and my lack of experience, I still knew what a prostitute was!

I don't know if I felt more angry or betrayed. I got into Ray's van, tossed the envelope at him, and didn't say a word. Ray opened the envelope, pulled out a twenty, and handed it to me. I looked at him and said, "Thanks."

To this day, I can't believe I said that.

I said thanks.

I shook my head. I thought, *You dumbshit, Kevin.*

Ray paid me no mind as he drove around. I had no idea where he was planning to go, and was unsure whether he'd want me to do it all again at another man's house with a different guy. But then he slowed the van, approached a stoplight, and clicked off the AM radio that had been blaring out Elton John's "Goodbye, Yellow Brick Road." The speakers slipped to silence just as Elton was singing one of those great lines: *"I'm not a present for your friends to open ..."* I remember it, because when I hear that song today, it has a new meaning for me. The song tells me who I had once been. And about who I had become.

I suddenly realized that Ray had stopped the van. We were at the entrance to a park. The Faggin' Wagon idled with a putt-putt-putt and Ray looked straight ahead.

"I'm going to drop you off at Tower Grove Park while I go do some business."

Panic!

"No Ray, I want to stay with you! Take me home. I don't want to be all alone!"

"Don't be such a fucking pussy! You won't be by yourself. I'm leaving you with a couple of guys about your age. Don't worry, you'll get along with them just fine; you'll have a good time. Now buck up and do as I say!"

I didn't know who these new guys were. I was scared. Little did I know that I was about to meet two people who would change my life forever and give me something I never thought I'd have—something I never expected to find in the hell I was now in.

Friends

The evening after I was first pimped out, Ray pulled his van into Tower Grove Park in south St. Louis. He drove around a big circle in the middle of the park, which was like a roundabout for cars to drop off passengers. As we looped around the other side, I saw what looked like a pavilion, some sort of Greek-looking building with pillars on the front. As we pulled around, I noticed a couple of kids sitting on the curb as if they were waiting for someone or something. When they saw the van, they both stood up. I figured they knew the van–and Ray.

Ray rolled down his window with a few cranks on the handle. "Hey, Stevie."

The taller boy approached the van. He appeared older than me and looked confident, like he knew how to handle himself.

Stevie glanced at me in the passenger seat. He rolled his eyes.

"Aw fuck, Ray, *another* one?"

"Yeah, Stevie … another one," Ray said. Without missing a beat, he continued, "This is Kevin. I need you to look after him while I go out; show him what's going on, will you?"

I immediately could tell that this kid Stevie had a comfortable enough relationship with Ray that he could talk back to him.

Stevie paused and then said, "Fuck you, Ray! Why don't you do him a favor and take him back to where you found him?"

While Stevie and Ray argued, I was thinking: *I'm in deep shit. These are the kids Ray wants to leave me with? I am in deep shit.*

As the back-and-forth between them continued, the other kid, who looked to be about my age, walked around to my side of the van and looked at me through my open window. I looked back at him and he smiled at me. He had long, wavy, unkempt blond hair and buckteeth–maybe it was just an overbite. His beautiful blue eyes were distant yet full of life.

Before I could crank up the window he said cheerfully, "Hi, I'm Squirrel." He pronounced it *Shquirrel*. "What's your name?" he asked.

As cranky and scared as I was, I immediately liked Squirrel. He was too lovable and comical to not like immediately.

I gave a weak smile and said in a whispery voice, "Um, hi. I'm Kevin."

"He can shtay with us!" Squirrel yelled, cutting into the bickering on the other side of the van. Then he looked at Stevie with a *can-I-keep-him-please* expression on his face.

"I'll stay here. I don't mind," I said. I think I actually surprised Ray.

Ray and Stevie glanced at each other, and as they shrugged off whatever disagreement they previously had, I opened the van's creaky passenger door. I stepped out and sat down on the curb. Ray flashed me a stern look, shifted the van to drive, and pulled away from the park.

TOWER GROVE Park is a city park in the southwest corner of St. Louis. Today, the area neighborhoods have gentrified gracefully and the park is quite beautiful. It is filled with lovely flower gardens, and certain sections of the park are made to evoke ancient Greek or Roman ruins. But in 1975, it was a rough area. By rough, I mean you had to be careful walking around after dark, especially if you were alone. I soon realized that the park was also famous for playing host to many young male hustlers. Even though I came to recognize many familiar faces lingering around over the next few months, I never really got to know any others except Stevie and Squirrel.

SO THERE I was, sitting between Stevie and Squirrel on the curb of the circle in Tower Grove Park. Squirrel sat very close to me. He hooked his arm in mine as he chatted away, doing his best to make me feel more at home. He began asking me a flurry of questions: "Where do you go to school? Do you collect baseball cards? Have you ever been to Courtesy? I like their malts. Do you?"

As I got to know him, I came to understand that Squirrel was unembarrassedly a demonstrative, affectionate person, not unlike a small child. Whenever he spoke, he would take hold of my arm or my hand, or would just simply lay his head on my shoulder. At this time, we were arm in arm. It made me feel strange at first, but I got used to it quickly.

Squirrel had a high-pitched, squeaky voice (our voices hadn't even changed yet) and a classic south St. Louis accent. For instance, he pronounced the word *four* as *far*. Like, *I'm driving down highway farty-far*. We would eat meals with a *fark*. Squirrel and I had similar accents and ways of saying things. We drank *soda*. We ate ice cream *sundas*, but if we went to church, it was on a *Sun-day*. Get in *that over there* sounded like get in *dat over dere*. Stevie's accent was different. It definitely wasn't a St. Louis accent. When he talked, it sounded more southwestern—what I imagined to be a Texas or Oklahoma twang. Stevie also looked different than Squirrel. He was taller, more muscular, and handsome, while Squirrel was just cute. Stevie's look was a cross between a high school football star and Mick Jagger. Later, I saw that from time to time he liked to wear overalls without a shirt. Not because he was from the country, but because when he did, people could see how well he was built. Normally, he would wear a pair of Levi's bell-bottom jeans and a T-shirt. He had brown mid-length hair.

As Squirrel chatted away, interrogating me about my life, Stevie sat there transfixed; he seemed to be enjoying Squirrel's friendly grilling. When I finally could get a word in edgewise, I said that I went to Hazelwood Junior High.

"What?!" Stevie yelled. "You live out *there*? Kid, what the hell are you doing all the way in the city?!"

Squirrel seemed confused. "What? Why? Where's that?"

Stevie ignored him and continued, "You don't belong here, kid. That's all I got to say."

This halted the conversation for an uncomfortable moment. *If I don't belong, then what am I doing here?*

I cleared my throat and the silence receded.

I said, "So, Stevie … where do you go to school?"

"I don't."

"How old are you?"

"Sixteen."

"Do you ever–"

"You done asking questions?"

"Yeah. Sorry." I wasn't sorry though. I guess I wanted to know where this was all leading. Before I could add anything, Stevie decided to ask me his own question.

"Where did Ray take you tonight?"

"Some guy named Jim."

The two guys looked at each other, smiled, and shook their heads.

"Nice house with a big kitchen?" Stevie asked. I nodded.

Stevie said with disgust in his voice, "Yeah, I know that guy."

"Oh, yeah?" I said. At least I had something in common with these boys.

"Did he want to do it on his kid's bed?" Squirrel asked.

I assume Squirrel asked the question already knowing the answer. I suppose he wanted to confirm in his mind that I found it just as repulsive as he did.

"Yeah, he did," I said. "The guy must be pretty rich, having a big house and all."

Stevie said, matter-of-factly, "He is. He's a lawyer, you know." He added, "You know what a lawyer is?"

"Yeah, I know what a lawyer is," I said, without knowing the whole of it.

I wanted to come across as confident. But I'm pretty sure both those guys could see through that. They were tough St. Louis kids. City kids. They knew what the world was about. I didn't know the whole story then, but it grew increasingly evident as I spent time with them.

AS FOR ME, all I did was worry. The thing that helped get me through was a silver-plated cross hanging from a silver chain I always wore around my neck. That first night I spent with my new friends was the first time I remember rubbing it.

A year earlier, my mom and I had been shopping together for clothes, when I found myself looking at a jewelry counter. What grabbed my attention was that silver cross necklace. It was pretty and simple—no adornments, just a shiny silver cross. My mom saw how much I liked it, and even though she was normally pretty frugal, decided to buy it for me.

Even then I had an interest in the divine, even religion. I remember being around twelve or thirteen when it dawned on me that the universe is without end, boundless. That usually scares people, but for me it made all things possible. If the universe is infinite, I'm a part of something bigger, something without end. I realized, like many people, that there was a connection between us and the Infinite, some purpose for existence.

I remember my first time seeing an image of Jesus. It was a painting hanging on a wall at my grandma's house, a graphic depiction of Jesus dying on the cross. I think Grandma was trying to teach me who Jesus was and that I should love him. It failed to dawn on her that an image of a horribly brutalized and bloody man being executed on a cross might not be the best evangelism for a four-year-old kid. It wasn't a nuanced approach, but it was what she thought she was supposed to do.

Little did I realize that image of suffering would eventually be the reason I could later accept and understand Jesus as God, *my God*. The idea that a man who took on suffering was God later fascinated me and, ultimately, comforted me. Maybe Grandma wasn't so wrong in her approach after all.

I wore the shiny new cross around my neck constantly and took special care of it. The night after my first "trick," sitting there and talking with Stevie and Squirrel, I remember holding that cross between my thumb and forefinger. I rubbed it for comfort. By the end of that summer, I had worn most of the silver off the cross, right down to the brass underneath.

STEVIE, SQUIRREL, AND I sat talking that evening as the sun set. Around dusk, a car drove around the circle and parked a distance from the three of us. The car's engine idled steadily for a moment and then its headlights went out. A middle-aged man exited, walked in our direction, and looked right at us while he approached. He walked past us toward the pavilion.

Squirrel looked at Stevie.

Stevie said, "Yeah … go ahead."

Stevie looked at me and said, "You. Go with him."

Squirrel seemed to agree. He said, "Yeah, come on … some of them like it when another kid watches."

I wasn't exactly sure what he was talking about, but I followed him. The two of us went across the pavilion next to the fountain, then over to the men's restroom. As soon as I entered, I noticed the sinks; one was clogged and overflowing, with water spilling onto the floor. To the right were two sets of old, stained urinals, three on each side. In the back were some stalls that were covered with spray paint and graffiti.

As Squirrel and the man walked toward the stalls, I heard Squirrel ask him something.

"You, me? Or me, you?"

The man said in a gruff, nervous tone, "You do me."

Squirrel responded in a monotone voice, almost automatically: "Twenty-five bucks."

Squirrel went to work right in front of me.

This was now officially the strangest day of my young life.

I eventually turned my back as Squirrel finished, which was evident by the sounds I was hearing. It was disconcerting, but I think what really bothered me was the way the strange man was touching Squirrel. The guy stroked his hair while Squirrel did his business. It was a sign of affection, but it was fake; it was only a pretense of what people who really love each other do. I didn't like seeing it. It made me mad. The guy shouldn't even have been touching anyone Squirrel's age, but it was the fact that he was touching *him* that turned my stomach. The man finally left the stall and walked past me, followed by a smiling Squirrel holding up twenty-five dollars—his hard-earned reward.

As we walked out, I noticed that there was something matting up Squirrel's hair. Stevie was waiting for us as we came out of the men's room, and as soon as he saw Squirrel, he said in a peculiar, almost motherly, voice, "Dammit, Squirrel, you've got cum in your hair!" Stevie took Squirrel's arm and led him back into the restroom. Like a mother caring for her child, Stevie held Squirrel's head over the sink and gently washed his hair with the restroom hand soap. The scene resembled a pastor baptizing a kid at church, except for the fact that Stevie kept cursing at Squirrel.

"There you go, kid," Stevie said, pulling several paper towels from a dispenser, handing them to Squirrel.

"Thanks." Squirrel smiled.

I REALIZE NOW, of course, that the day I had just experienced should not be a day ever experienced by any kid. There was nothing normal about it. But, for some reason, I felt at home with Stevie and Squirrel. I knew what they did, they both knew what I did, and we were all

OK with each other. That was priceless. When I saw the kindness and tenderness that Stevie showed to Squirrel as he washed his hair, I knew these were the friends I had always dreamed of having. This was love and compassion, even in the hellish circumstances around us. When I think back, I realize that my understanding of grace was forged in my ordeal with those two boys.

Two Lives

My brief foray into underage gay hustling was just one part of my life that summer. I also continued to carry on as a normal north St. Louis County suburban kid. I played the part of a straight, nerdy teenager well.

There were plenty of weekends that summer where I didn't hook up with Ray or go hustling in Tower Grove. Instead I spent time with kids in my neighborhood, doing normal kid things—you know, playing pretend wars, riding our bikes, getting ice cream. I also spent a lot of time with my family, even going on a vacation with them.

One day, my old man informed me that he'd be giving me a special treat.

"Hey, sport … I got a surprise for you!"

My ears perked. "Really? What?"

"I'm gonna take you to the circus!"

My dad was a busy guy. He worked long hours for an insurance office. He had been a chiropractor, but he wasn't making enough in his practice in Missouri, so he switched jobs. Yet he still found time to spend with the family and with me.

"Come on," my dad said, "it'll be fun. It's Barnum and Bailey. They're a classic!"

"I don't wanna go, Dad. Can't we do something else? Isn't there a Cardinals game we can head to this weekend? The circus is dumb!"

"Nope. I got tickets. Been planning it for a while. Gotta get my boy to the circus."

Like any normal kid, I dragged my feet and complained, but my dad prevailed. I eventually relented.

ONCE WE GOT to the circus and finally took our seats under the big top, I was feeling sorer than ever. The thought that I could possibly be away from my family, spending time with my real friends, didn't make my time at the circus any easier.

We waited around while the other people poured into the bleachers. I kept seeing much younger kids come in with their parents or friends. I thought to myself: *This is punishment. Real punishment worse than a grounding. Why the hell do I have to suffer through this?*

Two cowboys and a cowgirl came charging through the entrance to the big top to the left, a spotlight highlighting their way. The spot shifted to the center ring, highlighting a guy in a top hat. The ringmaster raised one hand, signaling the crowd to rise. His spoke into the microphone he was holding with his other hand: "La-dies and Gennnnntlemen! Please rise for the singing of our national anthem, *The Star-Spangled Banner*!"

The crowd of people all around me stood, including my dad. He grabbed ahold of my arm, yanking me upward to stand for the song. The whole time, I kept thinking to myself how stupid everyone else was for having to stand for a song. Who cared that it was our national song? It didn't belong there. Sports events? A Cardinals game? Sure. That was something important. This was just dumb. A spectacle for kids. A stupid circus. *And why is Dad being so goddamn gruff with me? It's just a damn kids' show!*

When the clowns stepped into the center ring and pulled out balloons to make funny animal shapes, I nearly lost it. I stood up to go. Anywhere really. I wanted to get away from there. My old man pulled me back down on my butt, looked at me sternly, and whispered to me, "Hey. Give it a chance ..."

Right after the clowns, a spotlight flared high above us, revealing a huge, ball-shaped metal cage. I heard the high-pitched growl of two motorcycles. The cage door to the giant sphere opened and the two cyclists drove their machines inside. As the cycles chased each other, screaming around like two enraged wildcats, I felt my stomach tense from excitement. This actually was pretty cool. When the third cyclist entered I thought I was going to scream. Wow! It really was something else.

The show went on, as the show must always go on. First, the animals came out. Lions and tigers. Then there was another clown act. This time they tickled me with their antics. And before I knew it, the show was over and I was smiling. My dad was right. The circus *was* fun. It took me in, and for a bit, my identity–the dark side of my other life–didn't matter. I was only a kid again, sitting with his dad, enjoying a fun family show.

I thanked my dad in the car. He smiled and drove the two of us back home. Today, I wonder how my parents–two loving people–might have reacted if I'd told them that I was gay. My guess is that, given their level-headedness, they probably would have "gotten me help." But I didn't need help. This much I knew about myself. Like so many kids, what I needed was to be told I wasn't an "aberration" to be "corrected."

Still, something held me back from telling my parents: the fear of losing everything if they knew the whole story. What else could I believe? I'd seen the fallout other gay people suffered. I knew that revealing I was gay would bring all the weight of society's judgment against me. And I wasn't going to go through that.

ANYTIME I WANTED to see Stevie and Squirrel, all I had to do was get on the phone with Ray. This method of communication gave me the impression that I was the one controlling my alternative life. After all, couldn't I just hang up or tell Ray no?

Ray never failed to pick me up. He'd always ask how long I could hang with him, and then get me back to my neighborhood. Once, I even asked my mom and dad if it would be OK if I spent a few days with a friend and his family at their cabin near the Meramec River. You know, an all-American, fun-filled week canoeing and playing in the water. Instead, I spent the five-day stretch running with Stevie and Squirrel, in and around the city. The three of us would hang out at Tower Grove in the evenings, and sleep over at an adult friend of Stevie's when we were finished. My mom and dad believed my story.

And I thought I was getting away with something.

DURING THAT TIME, Squirrel, Stevie, and I often went to Forest Park, which housed the St. Louis Zoo, an outdoor theater, and an art museum. Forest Park sat to the northwest of Tower Grove Park. For us, it was more of a hangout spot, not a place where we could carry out our hustling "work," though older guys would hustle there at night. During the daytime, it was a place for families to barbecue and kids on school outings to explore the zoo or planetarium.

The places at Forest Park were great because the zoo and art museum had free admission.

Like excited students, the first thing Squirrel and I always wanted to see was "Black Toe," an Egyptian mummy on display at the art museum in a big glass case. Yet one day Stevie wouldn't have it.

"Where you guys running off to?" he asked.

"We want to see Black Toe," I said.

"OK. But there's a load of other things to see besides a dead Egyptian guy. Follow me."

Squirrel and I looked at each other and did what we knew we needed to do. We listened and obeyed. We took a left into the medieval area. As soon as we entered, we saw an old stone slab with a picture of a boy and girl in medieval garb. The entire thing had old German script written around it.

"What's this?" Squirrel asked. "Who are those kids?"

Stevie read the placard. "It's a tombstone," he said. "Those two are brother and sister, and they died when they were only fourteen."

"Why'd they die?" Squirrel asked. "They're so beautiful …"

"They died of the plague or something …"

It was so sad. Two kids, a brother and sister, dead. I thought about it and it bothered me. It still does. I remember how Squirrel turned to me and looked like he might cry. He was the first to speak.

"That ain't right," he said. "Fourteen-year-olds shouldn't die." The image haunted me.

Some of the other rooms in the museum weren't too interesting. Old, dark paintings usually didn't catch our attention. But when we got to the impressionist paintings by artists like Monet, Seurat, and Van Gogh, we were all fascinated, especially Stevie. Squirrel and I studied Seurat's works particularly closely; we were fascinated with his style and the way the little dots formed a whole. But one day we got too close. A security guard on duty began to walk in our direction and shouted, "Hey! You kids. Get away from there."

Stevie grabbed us by our collars and pulled us back.

"Watch out, guys. You're gonna get us kicked out."

We backed off and moved to the next room.

"Come on, Stevie!" Squirrel and I said together. "Take us to Black Toe!"

"*Fuck* … you two. All right," Stevie said.

Stevie guided us down a stairwell in one corner of the building, and we followed closely behind. Although Squirrel and I tended to get lost on the way to Black Toe, Stevie apparently knew the way. The museum was fairly empty that day. The reason I remember that fact is because of what happened next.

"Hey Kevin, come back here," Squirrel whispered to me in the stairwell as Stevie went ahead.

"What?" I asked.

"Come *here*," he said. He pulled on my jean jacket, drawing me close to him. I saw him smile.

He gave me a kiss. A peck on my lips. Then he hugged me. I smiled at him and felt warm inside. It wasn't like any of the encounters I'd had with the other guys. No, it was pure. Innocent. Playful. It was love.

"Come *on*, you two!" Stevie yelled from the bottom of the stairwell.

Squirrel took my hand and pulled me as he took off with a run. I followed. We turned the corner and we finally saw him. The mummy, that is.

Like I said, I'd seen the mummy before. But this time was different, because Stevie gave us a little lesson. He told us about Egypt, how the priests were the ones to make the mummies, and how they'd pull the corpse's brain through the nose with a special tool. It was fascinating. Stevie had so much knowledge about stuff. I looked up to him.

"That's the thing, though …" Stevie said, drifting off.

"What? What's the thing?" I asked.

"This is where all of us end up," Squirrel said, making me think he'd heard Stevie say this before.

"Where all of us end up? As mummies?" I was still oblivious to the point of the conversation.

Stevie said, "No Kevin. We all end up here: we all die. It don't matter if we end up as a mummy, or we're buried six under, or we're burned in a funeral pyre. All we got is today. But, all in all, me 'n you and ol' Black Toe here are all in the same boat."

I stared at the mummy for some time. Squirrel and Stevie wandered off to the next room, where other Egyptian artifacts sat in glass cases. Finally, I joined my friends.

ONE MUGGY JUNE day a few days after our visit to the museum, I accompanied Stevie and Squirrel to the St. Louis Zoo, which is also in Forest Park. It was very hot that day and unfortunately, I was wearing super dark blue jeans. My legs seemed to soak up the summer sun and heat. I felt heavy and complained a lot. It didn't help that Missouri humidity turns sweat into a totally useless byproduct that has no purpose other than sticking to your clothes and skin.

Stevie said we were going to see some birds. But I didn't want to see birds. I wanted to soak my shirt with water and ride the miniature train in the shade with Squirrel.

Why in the world would he want to go see birds, anyway? We see birds every day in the park.

"Come on, Stevie. I'm tired. Can't we at least sit down for a while?" I asked.

"Keep up, Kev. We're not far. You'll forget yourself once you see this. It's downright cool."

"I don't know why you want to see a bunch of dumb birds, anyway ..." I stopped walking, and added, "Why? What're we going for?"

Stevie stopped abruptly and turned to me. "How do you expect to ever make it in life, Kevin? Hmmm?"

"Uh ... what do you mean?"

"I mean ... I mean to say ... *here we are!* Look at this! We're in the Saint fucking Louis Zoo! This life's bigger than having fun just to have fun." He swayed when he spoke and gesticulated wildly. "Sometimes, you have to put in a little effort to find yourself ... *in wonder.*"

Both Squirrel and I were used to listening to Stevie's many rants. More often than not they were fueled not only by his passion on a given subject, but also by a 40-ounce bottle of malt liquor beer that he drank out of a brown paper bag. He often consumed these en masse, gulping them down before we went in the zoo or any other place. At that time, he was fairly plowed. He had polished off two before our trip that day, an inconvenience not only because of his rants, but the effect the booze had on his bladder. He was always stopping to piss and it annoyed us.

Stevie turned and headed away from us. I looked at Squirrel, who shrugged at me and proceeded to follow Stevie. Squirrel wasn't happy, I could tell. But he followed Stevie anyway. What else was he going to do? Stevie was buzzed pretty hard, but what he said had weight. That didn't mean that I had to like it.

Find yourself in wonder. Uh-huh. Yeah, right.

I soldiered on, continuing my trek across the big grounds of the zoo, following our dogged, determined, and drunken leader.

I caught up and we walked through the humidity for what seemed like ages. As we came around the bend, Stevie pointed to a structure in the distance and said, "Here we are."

It's about damn time …

There, in a corner of the zoo surrounded by a mess of weeds and unkempt trees, stood an enormous black cage. It was metal and built in the shape of a dome. It must have been forty or fifty feet high and at least twice that distance wide. As we got closer, Squirrel's pace quickened to catch up to Stevie, whose determination never faltered after chewing me out.

As I neared the bars of the big cage, I could hear dozens of birds fluttering and chirping inside. People entered through a passageway, a caged room with doors on both ends, so the birds wouldn't escape as folks went into the main enclosure.

"Av-ee-air-ee …" Squirrel mouthed, reading the black-and-white placard.

"Right," Stevie said. "It's where they keep the birds. The aviary!"

As I walked into the large cage, I looked at Stevie raising his arms high in the sky, his hands spread out like he was trying to catch the air. Squirrel did the same. Then I did. The birds kept swooping down to the children, who were throwing handfuls of bird feed. Their parents had procured the feed for them from shiny red dime dispensers at the cage entrance. As the flocks went by, I could feel the air rush past my arms. I remember thinking the birds were like magic sprites or spirits, with all their different colors. They flicked and flapped by us, dodging right and zigzagging left. I smiled. And Stevie, even with all his alcohol-soaked fulminations, was right– this was a wonder worth seeing.

We played around in the cage for a while. The other adults didn't pay us much attention. Stevie could have been an older brother or cousin. If they thought of it at all, they probably figured our parents left us at the zoo. In that day, it wasn't out of the ordinary. We got to be free enough to be on our own. At the same time, we were kids, plain and simple. We goofed off. We jumped and danced. In the deep Missouri heat of that day, we had fun–so much fun, that I'd forgotten how miserable I thought I'd been.

After the aviary, even Stevie seemed winded. We walked a few dozen yards to a single water fountain nearly overrun with thirsty kids. When I finally got to the water stream, Squirrel put his face down. I waited a moment to allow him to drink. "Just drink," he said. I could see Squirrel's mouth next to mine, slurping the water.

After a minute or two we heard an older boy yell, "Come on! Quit hogging the water, *fags*!" He pushed us apart and away from the fountain.

"Did you get enough?" Squirrel asked.

"Yeah. It's OK. Come on. Let's go sit in the shade." I hadn't had enough to drink, but the older boy threatened me–not only because he pushed us away, but also because of what he called us. I just wanted to get away.

I could see Stevie sitting under a tree, on a park bench on the zoo grounds. Squirrel and I decided to join him. We sat in silence next to him for several minutes, enjoying the cool shadow cast by the tree's canopy. The sweat dripped off our heads.

"Do you know that metal cage–the Aviary–was actually built for the 1904 World's Fair in Saint Louis, Missouri?" Stevie asked. He said *St. Louis* differently than Squirrel or I would; it's like he blended the two words together. Quirks like that stuck in my head.

I wasn't surprised when Stevie told us about the history of the Aviary. He seemed to be a font of knowledge. To me at least he did; Squirrel seemed to be off in his own world whenever Stevie taught us about things, his attention floating away like a butterfly.

"The *Laweesiana Exposition*!" Stevie hollered out as if it was the title of a TV show and he was the announcer.

"What?"

"The. Louisiana. Exposition," he said very clearly. "That's what they called it for real. But we know it as the 1904 World's Fair. It was on the grounds of Forest Park. You know–*our* Forest Park. One of the biggest fairs ever, they said. They had wonders there that would have blown your mind. That same year, ol' Saint Louie got the Olympics too. Bet you didn't know all that, Kev."

"No, Stevie, I didn't."

Stevie, our unofficial adult, was tight lipped about who he was or where he came from, but he seemed educated. Maybe it was just natural intelligence. Despite his circumstances, he took notice of beautiful things and good people. I have to be honest that I had a crush on Stevie from the beginning, but the physical attraction morphed into a form of hero worship.

STEVIE DIDN'T HAVE a home, but he always seemed to have a place to stay–Sam's. When my parents thought I was camping and I stayed with Squirrel and Stevie, we stayed at Sam's.

I should say: Stevie stayed *with* Sam.

Stevie, Squirrel, and I stayed at Sam's that day we went to the zoo, and we were all exhausted. Though we spent many days walking all over the city, from park to park, that day in particular stands out, because it was so damn hot. Occasionally we'd hitchhike to get to the other side of the city. But most of the time we just walked. That day, I remember that we had walked a lot. In reality, Sam's house wasn't that far, but it sure seemed like it that day. When we finally got to the safety of Sam's house, we were tired. Stevie wanted us to sleep and went to bed in Sam's room. I lay down next to Squirrel.

The two of us lay side by side, facing each other on the floor in front of a plaid sofa that Stevie called a davenport. I always thought that was a weird word for a piece of furniture, perhaps something my grandpa would say. We called it a sofa.

We lay there giggling like two schoolgirls, telling jokes, laughing so much that Stevie came out and told us to shut up. We got quiet quickly, but it only lasted for a minute before we were back at it. From the very beginning, since our first night at Tower Grove, Squirrel and I had a strong connection and an unspoken language between us. We were always free to be exactly who we were with each other. He was fun and playful, a child. We thought in the same way, had the same ideas. I knew during the first stay at Sam's that Squirrel was more than a buddy. He was my first love.

As we lay on the floor laughing, Stevie and Sam finally gave up trying to make us sleep. They put on a record to drown out our voices. Squirrel loved to dance, so he got up and swayed and rocked, and I felt my muscles loosen and the fear melt away.

"Come on! Kevin, get up and dance. Dance with me!" he said, extending his hands to come into mine.

"OK." I danced. I listened to Lou Reed chant the lyrics of "Transformer" as the piano and guitar cranked out a tune.

We collapsed after the song and fell to the floor. We had turned off the lights, but I could still see Squirrel. I looked into his eyes and took in his face. Squirrel had beautiful round eyes that were a kind of hazy blue. His nose wasn't pointy or large or small, just perfect for the rest of his face. I think the one thing that stuck out–literally–on Squirrel was the angle of his teeth. I'm sure this is why he was called Squirrel, but it didn't bother me. His smile made up for those goofy choppers. When he smiled, it was the brightest thing in my world.

Squirrel was skinny and wore clothes that were a couple of sizes too big. Like the rest of us, he would stick with the same limited wardrobe throughout the week. He loved to wear a baggy old army shirt over a colored T-shirt. I never saw him wear jeans, but always something that resembled brown or blue work pants with sneakers at the bottom.

That night, his clothes lay in a messy pile next to mine on the opposite side of the couch. He smelled like cigarettes. He always did. He smoked, though not often. As we lay there, talking quietly, I breathed in his musky smell mingled with notes of tobacco, sweat, and Pixy Stix.

Both Squirrel and I loved the long tubes of colored sugar, which were always topped with a SweeTart. On that evening, before we came to the house to rest, we had bought a Pixy Stix to share between us. We had argued over who was to get the SweeTart in a playful, mocking way. This time, he insisted that I get the SweeTart. But I was insistent that he should have it. We went back and forth like this for a while, annoying the hell out of Stevie in the process. Eventually, we both relented and we split the Pixy Stix between us. He'd take a swig of the sugar from the cheap plastic tube and pass it to me. Then, when the last of the tube's sugar had been emptied into our watering, candied mouths, we broke the sweet and tart chunk of sugar with a *click-snap* between Squirrel's fingers. He gave me one half and I took the other.

When I think about that evening, and us lying together on the floor, I remember the sweetness hanging on the edge of my tongue from earlier that day at the museum as Squirrel looked in my eyes and gave me a peck on my lips. Touching my shoulder, he pulled me closer to him.

He asked, "Why won't you kiss me? I like to kiss you."

I wouldn't allow any of the men I went off with to kiss me. Part of it was that I didn't know how. I hadn't had the experience of authentic intimacy. But it was also a place I didn't want to go with those guys; at least I could keep *that* for myself.

Yet now, lying on the floor alone with Squirrel, I felt my face get hot and red.

"I don't know how," I said. I shrugged my shoulders, shying away.

He pulled me closer.

"Don't worry. I'll teach you," he said, smiling.

And he did. As we embraced, our tongues entwined and our lips sealed together. It was a weird blend of cigarettes, Squirrel's musky essence, and Pixy Stix. It was no doubt strange, but good and pure. Still, I had fears. Maybe those fears were wrong, but they had been engrained into me … no, more like *pounded* into me by my church, my family, what I saw and heard on TV. The messages against *who I was* were everywhere.

In fact, just weeks before all this happened, I'd heard a reading at church that seemed to directly target all of us. The passage was from the Bible, an excerpt from Paul's letter to the Romans in the New Testament. I remember the lector reading how God gave some over to wickedness. When the lector read the part where men exchanged *natural* relations for *unnatural*, I remember him looking up after he said the word *unnatural*. It was as if he was saying it directly to me. I was the condemned.

After Squirrel and I had kissed awhile I stopped and looked up at him. "Man, God is really going to hate us for this."

He looked puzzled and cocked his head. "God doesn't hate us; he likes us."

"Really? Why?"

"Because we're nice. God doesn't hate nice people." And then he continued to kiss me.

I remember thinking that I'd never forget the smell or the taste of that evening, together with Squirrel on the floor. And I haven't.

Learning the Ropes

"Awww ... Kev ... *Fuck off!*"

It was the morning after Squirrel and I had kissed at Sam's, and the sun was beginning to peek through Sam's funky orange curtains. Its light cast a dull amber glow on the nicotine-stained walls.

"What do you mean? Me? Fuck off?" I asked Squirrel. I stood next to the television, fiddling with the large plastic channel knob, trying to find a show to watch. These were the seventies: there was no remote control, so changing the channel took some motivation.

The day before, I'd felt like I had taken one step closer to adulthood, to independence or self-reliance. This morning, however, we were back to being little foul-mouthed, obnoxious boys who wanted their own way.

Annoyed, Squirrel stood up from the dirty carpet in the living room. He kicked his sleeping bag out of his way and made his way past me. He tramped to the clunky television, which was encased in wood veneer. The TV sat on the opposite side of the room under the window; it looked more like a piece of furniture than a piece of electronic equipment.

Squirrel grabbed the round channel dial and clicked it right several times. The screen snapped past three or four channels, with static buzzing through every channel shift. Squirrel found the channel he wanted and became happy again.

"There! Found it! We're watching this."

It was a rerun of Squirrel's favorite show, *The Banana Splits Adventure Hour*. It looked like it was in the first minutes of the program. A yellow title screen with bright orange lettering lit up the still-dim living room. Squirrel began chanting loudly, barking out the lyrics in sync with the song coming from the television: *"Two banana, four banana, one banana, three …"*

Squirrel loved the "goofy puppets," as he called them–the brightly colored polyester costumes the actors wore in the live-action part of the show. I thought the whole thing was stupid. It seemed to me that it was made for kids much younger than us. But my attempt to change the channel to something different was pointless; Squirrel was adamant about watching his show. Maybe hearing that music and chanting along with it made him feel more like a kid and less like a dirty park hustler.

I suffered through it just to appease him. But it was more than that: I liked it when he was happy. Even though I thought the show was dumb, watching his antics and the smile on his face made up for it. When the show was concluding, Stevie and Sam stepped into the living room.

Stevie stood behind us, glaring at the TV in apparent derision.

"You've got to be kidding me. *Banana Splits?*" he said.

I looked back at him, nodding and raising my eyebrows. Stevie got the picture that I was watching the show more out of tolerance than as a tried-and-true fan. He smiled.

"Shut up, guys! The theme song is coming on again," Squirrel said.

He began singing the lyrics in perfect unison with the TV as the credits rolled. I stood up and got dressed. Sam came in and gave me a friendly punch on the shoulder.

"Hey."

Sam was a good guy. His place was safe for us. He was older than we were–probably in his early twenties. I could tell that Stevie and Sam cared for each other. He wasn't like the other guys. Sam was one of the good ones. Over the summer, the refuge we found at his house would turn out to be a godsend.

While I was dressing, Sam said he had to be somewhere and told Stevie to lock up before we left.

"What's our plan for today?" I asked Stevie.

"I want to go get some beer," he said. "Kevin, you got any extra cash?"

"Yeah. Here you go."

Naturally, I had extra cash. I never wanted to keep any money I made off the customers and was happy to throw all of it in the kitty for what the three of us needed. I handed Stevie three crumpled-up twenties.

"Man! Kevin. How much do you have?" Squirrel asked.

"I don't know."

"Who cares?! Let's get out of here," Stevie said.

"Where're we going to go?" I asked.

"Don't worry. I've got a place," Stevie said.

Of course he had a place. All three of us would drink now and then, but drinking for Stevie was almost a daily activity, even in the morning. It bothered me sometimes, especially when he drank too much and his words slurred. But I knew why he did it. Even then I knew why he did it. It numbed him, covering up whatever pain was eating away at his insides.

Stevie led us outside and locked the door to Sam's house. We headed across the city earlier than usual.

"Look, here we are," Stevie said as he pointed to a corner liquor shop stuffed back in a residential area in south St. Louis.

"Can we come in too?" I asked.

"Yeah. Sure. Just don't be stupid," he warned.

Squirrel looked at me and flashed a wry smile. "Hey Kevin," he whispered, *"two banana, four banana, one banana, three ..."* With each count of "banana" he bounced up and down. Anyone seeing him couldn't help but smile over how cute he was. Ever see a kitten jump after a yarn ball? Squirrel was inherently cute.

Completely ignoring where we were and the inappropriateness of chanting a children's television show theme song while we tried to illegally obtain alcohol, I smiled and happily chimed in, singing: *"H. R. Pufnstuf! Who's your friend when things get rough?"*

It was an ongoing, playful argument that Squirrel and I had about which kids' TV show was better. His favorite show was *Banana Splits*; mine was *H. R. Pufnstuf.* The fact that he had just gotten his way at Sam's house with that morning's TV schedule only made him more determined to win this little competition between us. We had taken the *Banana Splits* vs. *H. R. Pufnstuf* argument as far as it would go; now we were just having fun with it. Squirrel head-butted me in rhythm as he sang, *"One banana, two banana, three banana, four!"* I countered more loudly with, *"H. R. Pufnstuf, who's your friend when things get rough?"* We laughed and laughed, not noticing that Stevie had taken his beer to the counter.

"Excuse me," Stevie said to the lady at the register. He grabbed the two of us and neatly deposited us outside the store, then went back inside to complete his purchase.

When Stevie came out, Squirrel had the guts to ask, "Did you get me anything?"

Stevie leered at both of us. But I knew he didn't mean it. I knew inside he was smiling. We were a family and we were his two boys. How could he not be anything but amused by us?

FROM THERE WE moved to Forest Park with Stevie's beer, careful to avoid any cops. He did share some of it with us, enough to give us all a buzz that lasted the rest of the afternoon. Stevie, naturally, had more than us, which translated into him needing to pee more often. Various stores served him well, and gave Squirrel and me the opportunity to goof off some more.

Squirrel had the uncanny ability to put me at ease wherever we found ourselves. He was so naturally playful. It's probably why I considered him to be the same age I was. You're only as old as your playfulness and your sense of wonder.

Even at Tower Grove Park, which is where we ended up that evening, the two of us could turn a hunting ground for sexual predators into our own playground. We loved to run through all the Victorian-style gazebos and shelters. We often played on the old stone blocks arranged to look like ancient ruins. Squirrel and I called them "The Castle." Squirrel had a vivid imagination; he would instruct me to stand on the ruins and then he'd attack the castle with a pretend sword and engage me in a mock sword fight. We'd end up laughing from exhaustion after the battle.

Ironically, I learned to love that park at night. It was macabre and gothic, like the set of a Vincent Price movie (today, I'd say it resembles one of Tim Burton's darker movies). Behind the pavilion was what looked like a long, open fairway that stretched all the way to Kingshighway Boulevard. Mature cottonwoods and elms bordered both sides. When the wind was blowing hard at night, causing the trees and their shadows to sway, it looked like a bunch of disembodied spirits were performing some sort of maniacal dance. We didn't have to be afraid of what lurked about because it was just us.

That night, in Tower Grove Park, Squirrel and I ran from side to side, pretending we were being blown about by the wind. Once again, we annoyed the hell out of Stevie, but when I remember it, it's as if the two of us were dancing with the spirits and each other.

Later that evening, after we had our fill of beer, the three of us walked up the grassy fairway. It was growing dark and the streetlights in the distance began to flicker on. The park itself was dark enough that my mind turned the whole affair into an adventure. Along with darkness, hunger crept up on us too. So we decided to go to another one of our haunts: the Courtesy Diner.

The Courtesy was a twenty-four-hour diner about a mile from Tower Grove Park. It was a groovy-looking, but simple, brick building. A plain white sign read **COURTESY DINER** in big blue block letters. We loved to go there at all hours. Not only because they were open late, but also because most of the staff tolerated us. Even though a few of the staff seemed to know who—and what—we were, and we had to tolerate the occasional jerk, it was still a good place to go to grab a bite to eat.

The inside of the Courtesy must have been only fifty feet long and half as wide. A row of round plastic-covered stools lined a counter. The space for the waitstaff and cooks to prepare meals, throw fries in boiling oil, take orders, and collect tabs couldn't have been more than three feet wide. No wonder many of the workers were crabby. The diner is still there today and relatively unchanged from how it was in 1975. I know their food is still great, as I've dined there several times since my time as a hustler.

When we sat in our booth, Squirrel slid up close to me. His simple act of physical contact was what I enjoyed more than anything else in the world.

Stevie started saying something. I didn't hear it, because I was so lost in the moment.

"Kevin … *Kevin!*"

"Huh? Yeah?"

"Can you sport us a ten? I'm hungry."

Again, I was buying dinner. It wasn't because Stevie or Squirrel didn't have any cash. I think it was because they knew that it was what I could do to help our little family.

"Hey, you! We're hungry!" Stevie commanded, lifting his arm and waving at the waitstaff leaning against the counter on the opposite side of the restaurant.

A tired-looking, middle-aged waitress looked our direction, then looked at the other waitress and scowled, shaking her head. She moseyed our way and walked around the counter with her head down. I felt a knot building in my gut.

She spoke with an Oakie or Arkansas lilt-and-swing that sounded more jeering than genteel: "You boys? *Again?*"

"That a problem?" Stevie shot back. His accent seemed to thicken in response to hers.

"Well ... no ... I s'pose not. It depends on what you boys are doing here at this hour. Don't you have no families worried about where you are? What you're *doing*?" She leaned on the table, trading glances between the three of us. I remember her eyes shifting to each one of us, one after another.

I felt embarrassed and exposed.

Squirrel surprised me by entering into the conversation, if you can call it that. He looked directly at her and said, "Ma'am, we're hungry."

"Oh!" The waitress showed a look of mock surprise. "You're *hungry*? That's why people come to the Courtesy Diner, ain't that so? To order their dinner. Well, boys, I tell you what. My shift ends at ten. That's in about fifteen minutes. I venture to guess that you can wait for my relief to take your order. I don't need no wild, pretty boys to jip me before I go home and have a nice, late meal with my own."

With that, she stuck her order pad and pencil in her front pocket, undid the ties on her apron, and walked away. As she left, she mumbled, *"Little faggots."*

The three of us looked at each other. Squirrel looked more surprised than insulted or shocked. But Stevie was mad.

"We don't want a bitch for a waitress, anyhow!" Stevie yelled far too loudly for his own good, or ours. This was out of character for him. Most of the time, we just walked out without incident and would try again later. Tonight was different, though. We were hungry.

"Shhhh!" I shushed him. "Let's don't get kicked out, OK? We still have to eat and I don't want some ol' gas station hot dog, OK?"

We never did get a meal at the Courtesy that night. Sometimes it's better to cut your losses before you get too far behind. Some cops showed up to eat, and it's not like there weren't other places we could go. Saint Louis is a big city, after all.

THE NEXT DAY, Stevie and Squirrel walked me through how to hustle the correct way at Tower Grove. Stevie figured if I was there, I might as well do it well. Maybe he thought I could make more cash too. It wasn't like he was using me like Ray. Not at all. Stevie wasn't like that. I think, more than anything else, he wanted me to be safe and for me get it over with quickly. He just wanted to show me the ropes, to learn how to be safe. Like any other job, hustling had its rules, regulations, and procedures. There just wasn't a manual.

If you were taking care of business in the men's restroom, it was easy. We always used the buddy system. Either Stevie or Squirrel would come along with me—usually Squirrel—and it always involved one of two acts. This was determined by using Squirrel's words: "You me, or me you?" If they did me it was fifteen bucks. If I did them, twenty-five bucks. With Stevie or Squirrel present, the johns were a lot less likely to screw me over on payment.

Taking care of business in a guy's car was a different matter altogether. Stevie told me right off the bat, "If you're going to do that, *always* talk to them through the passenger side window, and always, *ALWAYS* leave that window open, for a quick escape if you need it." That advice saved me more than once. It was the difference between being roughed up and having the pulp beat out of you.

Of course, there were also the dates that Ray would arrange for me. I would try to avoid those as best I could, but he was my ride, and also my access to Stevie and Squirrel. I was dependent on him. It was during this time that I learned in no uncertain terms that some of these guys were downright mean and could hurt you. In my experience, the mean ones almost always turned out to be cops. Cops had the power to arrest you, to send you off far away from your family and friends. Because of the power they had, they could extract whatever sexual favors they wanted from you without repercussion. And they could act as mean as they wanted.

Later that day, Ray's van pulled around the circle at Tower Grove Park. Squirrel and I were goofing off as usual, chasing each other. Stevie was tolerating us and had even gotten into it a little, cracking a smile when he caught me by the shirt. Suddenly, we heard the Faggin' Wagon, with its out-of-tune *put-putting* engine, turn and come around the circle. The window rolled down and I saw Ray's face. He had long since given up trying to impress or woo me with a syrupy smile or fake congeniality.

"Kevin!" He shouted from the van. "You're up."

My heart sank. One moment Squirrel and I were jumping on Stevie's back, goofing off like any kids should be doing in the summer. The next minute, I was a piece of meat for some random older guy to grope and fondle. I knew what was going down. It wasn't what I signed up for. The more I felt a love and connection with my friends, the more I knew I was trapped in Ray's snare. For me, it was an emotional conundrum.

Defeated, I sauntered over to the van, opened the door, and got in.

RAY DROPPED ME off at a house near the intersection of Nottingham Street and Kingshighway. I remember it still because of the street's name: Nottingham and all that Robin Hood stuff stuck in my head. I knocked on the door. The door lock unlatched and the door burst open.

The guy immediately grabbed me by my jean jacket and said, "Get in here, you little faggot!" His eyes were burning and angry. He knew what he was doing and wasn't afraid of anything or anyone.

What the hell was that all about?

"Get in here, dammit! Now listen, keep your mouth shut and do what you're told and you'll get out of here with your money. Do you understand?"

I said in a low voice, "Yeah."

"Yes … what?" He gave me a pop on the head.

"Yes … sir. *Yes, sir!*"

"Get in here. Stay put. I'll be right back."

I stayed put. While I stood there in his living room, I surveyed the scene, assessing that he was a family man—and a cop. It's not like I saw a uniform lying around, but there was a plaque with what looked like a badge. As the man walked down the hall toward his bathroom, I saw a small revolver on his waist. He took the pistol out and put it in an old wooden cabinet in a high drawer. The gun caught my attention, but I assumed that a cop couldn't hurt you unless you were breaking the law or something. That was my naive fourteen-year-old mind at work.

Before I knew what had happened, he charged out of his bathroom wearing only white briefs and carrying a jar of Vaseline. He grabbed me by the back of my hair, dragged me into a rear bedroom, and spun me around. He was strong, like a predator reaching out to grab its prey in one swift move. He ripped down my pants and forced himself into me. Then he wrapped his arm around my throat in a chokehold and pressed his whole weight against me. My eyes bugged out and I gasped. *He's killing me. I'm gonna die!*

I awoke on the floor by the side of the bed with my pants and underwear down around my ankles. At some point, I seemed to have passed out. My insides and my bottom hurt. And I had a *huge* headache. I thought I might have been choked so badly that I passed out from a lack of air.

When Ray came to pick me up, I didn't say a word. I hopped in his van and we rode together in silence for a few miles.

Finally Ray said, "Well, don't you have something for me?"
Not this time, Ray.

"That guy was fucking mean. No way, Ray. I'm keeping it. I'm keeping it all."

Ray stared at me, taking his eyes off the road. It made me uncomfortable, because I thought we might get in an accident. But I kept staring back. I was bound and determined to make it hurt for him where it counted—the money.

"Kev … you know … sometimes … Just give me the money. Give me the *goddamn money*!"

"No."

We continued to argue as we drove back to Tower Grove. Finally, I said what I'd always wanted to say to Ray: "Fuck off, Ray. I'm keeping it."

It was the first time I'd told an adult to fuck off. It wouldn't be the last time either. It felt good, but I was worried.

What's he going to do? Just hold on a little longer. He can't do this to you. Stand your ground.

By then, we were pulling into the Tower Grove circle. As we did, I could feel a sharp pain grabbing my insides. As we neared Stevie and Squirrel, I jumped out of the van. When my feet hit the ground, the pain erupted. I immediately doubled over with terrible cramps. I cried. I didn't give a shit about the tears on my face—I hurt!

Ray got out of the other side of the van. He was continuing to argue over the money.

"You fucking think you can talk to me like that?!"

Something happened then that I'd never forget: Stevie walked past me and circled the van. His back was straight, his chest out, and his shoulders confident and muscular. He walked right up to Ray and said only one word: "Stop."

He meant it too.

Ray stopped his ranting. He stopped walking toward me and looked at Stevie.

Squirrel fell down on his knees on the ground next to me, embracing me with his arms.

"Kevin, are you OK? Don't cry! Stevie, do something. Kevin's hurt!"

I was hurting and crying. But at the same time it felt good to have Squirrel comforting me and Stevie defending me. I could hear bits and pieces of Stevie chewing out Ray. It sounded more like a dad interrogating a neighborhood bully than a teen hustler standing up to his pimp.

"What did you do to him?!" Stevie yelled.

"Nothing. I just picked him up from a date, that's all."

"Who'd you take him to?"

"Uh … well. It was–"

I didn't catch what Ray said. I never did get to know that guy's name, nor do I ever wish to. To me, he is a nameless sex offender and an evil man.

I heard Stevie resolutely say, "Never again. That guy's a freak."

Ray started to stutter something, but Stevie stopped him.

"No! Never again!" he said, one hand pointing to the ground, the other hand clenched in a fist. Even in the dark, I could have sworn that the hand making a fist was nearly white, Stevie was clenching so hard.

Ray made his way around Stevie to where I was on the ground. He tried to put his hand on my shoulder, but Squirrel wouldn't let him. He asked if I was OK and I nodded. This wasn't compassion, though: Ray was concerned about losing a worker who provided him with cash, a widget in his "freaky factory."

"I'm sorry, Kevin," he said. "Go ahead and keep the money."

He got in his van. Before he left he leaned out and said, "I'll see you guys on Sunday."

Bingo, Ray. That you will. I'll be better by then and you'll be able to send me out again.

Stevie joined Squirrel in comforting me, but Stevie had a more pragmatic approach to comfort. He told me what I needed to do.

"You're cramping, yeah?"

"It feels like I need to take a shit really bad," I said. "Can you get me to the restroom? Make sure there's no one in it."

"That's exactly what you need to do. Can you walk?"

"I think so. Can you guys come in there with me?"

"Sure."

I didn't want some john hanging around for a blow job when we got in there. And I was a scared kid, so I wanted them nearby.

As Stevie and Squirrel walked me to the restroom, I heard Squirrel ask Stevie, "Is he going to be OK? We don't have to take him to the hospital, do we?"

I began to cry more when I heard this.

Stevie responded, "Shhhh! Shut up, Squirrel! He'll be fine."

They got me to the toilet and I sat down with one of them on each side. I did my business and it made me feel better. As I was about to flush, Stevie stopped me.

"Get up. I want to look at it."

I stood up as he inspected the stool.

"There's hardly any blood. You'll be fine."

I knew Stevie was no doctor, but hearing him say that made me feel a thousand times better.

AFTER I CLEANED up, I asked Stevie if we could go back to Sam's and watch TV.

Squirrel glanced at Stevie, who said to me, "I've only made twenty-five and Squirrel just has fifteen. Um … I want to help you, but, you know … We have to work. Squirrel has to make money, more money for–" Stevie stopped short. I don't know what he wanted to say, but I think it was important.

When I realized the guys needed to score more cash, I remembered the packet of money I'd kept all to myself.

"Oh yeah," I said. "I forgot. Here, you guys can have this." And I gave them the envelope that I'd held back from Ray.

Stevie looked in it and smiled widely, his eyes gaping, astonished.

"Let's get outta here!" he said. "I'll stop and pick up some beer on the way!"

There must have been at least a hundred and fifty bucks in there.

On the way to Sam's, Stevie and Squirrel noticed that I kept asking the same questions and saying the same thing over and over, slurring my words. It seemed that I was either completely traumatized from that night's events or my brain had been damaged by that jerk choking me.

That night, Stevie didn't sleep with Sam like he usually did: he slept with us. Stevie, my protector, was on one side, and Squirrel, my comforter, love, and best friend, was on the other. That night, I felt more surrounded by love than I ever had before, and certainly have ever since.

What I Needed

Not all of the dates Ray set up for me were like that, the one with the evil cop. In fact, that one was by far the worst. Some of them were actually "fun" to my fourteen-year-old mind. Some of the guys were nice; some were cold and indifferent. Some guys would want to know details about my life–where I lived and went to school. I'd never give them these details, of course. I guess some of them wanted to feel as if they were my friends and I was their lover. Who knows, maybe it made them feel less guilty about their actions. Maybe it turned them on. One repeat customer actually wanted me to go on a vacation with him down to Florida, which just sounded stupid, even to me. But they were all passing faces, pedophiles. Using me, then throwing me away.

I continued on like this deep into July. I was able to carry on two separate lives–one with the peace that came with being with Stevie and Squirrel, yet working as a child prostitute. The other left me with my thoughts and shame, yet gave me peace at home. Living both lives wasn't that hard. My friends and family back in Florissant had no awareness of my friends at Tower Grove. Sometimes I would talk to Stevie and Squirrel about my life and friends in Florissant. I cherished the perfect days where the three of us wouldn't do any hustling at all, and we'd hang out like regular kids.

The Courtesy Diner was our frequent refuge, though it depended on who was working there. I think to most of the people who worked there, we were just some kids from the neighborhood. To others, we were *those little faggots*. When we were hassled, we learned not to fight back. We didn't stand a chance anyway. We knew where we stood in the pecking order, and it wasn't on top or even in the middle.

We always ended up hustling back at Tower Grove, trying not to get beat up or used in a way we didn't want to be. I would always join in to turn tricks. I should mention I hate the phrase *turning tricks*. There was no *trick* about it. Or, maybe I was the one being *tricked*. Maybe that's why I hate the phrase.

I would usually do business in the restrooms. Every once in a while I would get in a car with a guy and do it there. One time late in July, while Stevie was in the restroom with Squirrel, I was alone, sitting on the curb. A car pulled up, turned off its engine, then flashed its lights on and off. I looked around to where some of the other kids were sitting to see if they were going to go take advantage of this, but no one was making a move toward the car. One of the other boys nodded to me, indicating that the score was mine. So off I went. The boys laughed as I stood and began walking toward the car.

What's so damn funny? I brushed it off, thinking I was being paranoid.

I was careful to follow Stevie's advice from a month prior. I ran his words through my head: *Do the deal through the passenger side window and always leave that window down!*

I did exactly that, and brokered the deal in the usual way. It looked like I was about to make twenty-five bucks. I got in the guy's car and he immediately threw a towel at me, evidently to spit in.

So, he's done this before. Check.

After it was done, I said to the guy, "That's twenty-five."

"Get lost, kid."

This flew in the face of all decency for me!

I said, "No, you said you'd give me twenty-five dollars." I was going to give most of it to Stevie and Squirrel anyway.

The gentleman then pulled out a badge. That's right, another cop. Ah yes … one of *St. Louis's finest*.

Perhaps the smart thing to do would have been to say: "Yes indeed, Officer, you have a pleasant evening," and get out of the car. But I hadn't forgotten my experience with the violent cop Ray had left me with. Thoughts of how the cops treated us at the Courtesy Diner flashed in my head. Instead of doing the smart thing, I said, "Fuck you. Give me my money!"

"You little piece of faggot shit! Fuck *YOU*!"

Our friendly neighborhood cop grabbed me by my jean jacket with one hand and started to beat the hell out of me with his other hand. A mixture of anger, fear, and adrenaline immediately flowed and burned through me. Somehow, I was able to break free, bail out the window, and run toward the pavilion. I turned around and yelled, "Fuck you, pig!"

A few of the other hustlers—all lost boys themselves—started laughing. Then I noticed the cop moving out of his car. Panicking, I ran the rest of the way to the pavilion, where I stopped at the restroom entrance and turned again, relieved to see that the cop had driven away.

Stevie and Squirrel had heard me yelling and cursing. They hurried out of the restroom, followed by a man. He considered the situation and decided that he had better hightail it out too.

I stood there babbling away at both Stevie and Squirrel, all the synapses in my brain firing like lightning, trying to explain what had just happened. Stevie said, "Kevin, do you know you're bleeding?"

I went in the restroom to look in the mirror. My nose was bleeding and a little stream of crimson trickled down my chin. I also had a small cut on my right eyebrow. (This left a tiny scar that remains today, a little reminder of my former life each morning when I look in the bathroom mirror.)

Once I was able to get the whole story out to my friends, it was obvious that both Stevie and Squirrel knew the cop. Stevie asked me, "Didn't any of the other guys warn you?"

"No." I pointed out the guy who'd told me to go ahead.

Stevie didn't say a word after that, but walked over to a group of guys who seemed to be enjoying what had happened. Without muttering a word, he threw a solitary punch toward the guy who'd sent me to the cop, knocking him out cold. To say I was impressed would be an understatement, but I also felt afraid.

STEVIE TOOK HIS role as the adult for our little group seriously. We were all friends, but looking back, I realize Stevie had to be the responsible grown-up. It's not like any of us ever talked about what our roles were, but Stevie always stepped up as the authority figure. For example, when Squirrel was heading home for the night, Stevie would say to him, "Y'all go straight home now."

Squirrel would nonchalantly shrug and say, "I will."

But Stevie wouldn't leave it at that: "Boy, you know I'll find out if you don't."

Squirrel would look at the ground and say, "I know."

The thing that gets me to this day is how we, like any "real" family members, tried to find our place within our little unit. The fact that we weren't related by blood didn't matter. What mattered was that we knew each other and accepted each other unconditionally. How we treated each other was the way family members should act with one another. I'm not idolizing our little group (perhaps I did then, but I was just fourteen), but Stevie, Squirrel, and I provided for each other the essential psychological needs that any person desires: the need to feel safe, comforted, and to belong, regardless of your identity or preferences.

My family back in the suburbs loved me. I didn't doubt that. The fear that they would reject me was real, though. If they were to really know who I was, I might be tossed out on the street. Stevie and Squirrel would never have rejected me. In that way, they were family even more than my blood relatives. The primal urge to feel accepted and loved unconditionally was so strong, that I was willing to put myself at risk by doing what I did that summer.

One late Saturday night, when the three of us were going our separate ways, Squirrel said he needed to be home for some reason or another. I remember thinking it had something to do with his mom. I never met Squirrel's mother, but I know that he lived with her. Squirrel wouldn't talk about his mom (or any other family he might have had), and I never asked. If I had to guess, I would assume that one of the reasons that he was out hustling was so that he could keep money in the house for food. He was providing for her.

I think now the reason why none of us asked details about each other's lives is that we didn't have to. Maybe we didn't want to. What we had–together–was precious. And we didn't want to lose it.

That night, Stevie had something going on with some other friends more his age, but he waited around with me for Ray after Squirrel left. By this time, I dreaded spending any time alone with Ray, and I'm sure Stevie could sense this. It wasn't that I was afraid of Ray himself, but I did fear the unknown–where he might take me or whose house he might drop me off at.

"So is Ray going to take you home?" asked Stevie.

"I don't know, Stevie. I don't know where he's going to take me."

Just then, Ray's van pulled around the circle at Tower Grove. As he came to a stop, I stood up and walked to the curb, waiting for Ray to pull up the Faggin' Wagon.

Stevie didn't say anything; he simply waited for Ray to stop, then walked up behind me. As I opened the door to the van, Stevie told me to get in the back. He jumped into the passenger seat and informed Ray, "I'm staying with you and Kevin tonight."

I don't know what kind of power Stevie had over this so-called "adult," because even though it was obvious that Ray wasn't pleased with this arrangement, he didn't say one word. He simply nodded.

We drove about twenty minutes until we came to a small house with a carport. After pulling in, Ray turned off the engine and announced, "Home sweet home." He jumped out, slamming the driver's side door behind him.

Stevie didn't move a muscle.

Since Stevie didn't move, I didn't move.

When Ray saw that we were staying put, he turned and said, "Well, aren't you guys coming in?"

"That's OK, Ray–me and Kevin will sleep out here."

At that point, it was about three in the morning. Stevie and I were tired. We went to the back of the van and got ready for bed. Stevie stripped down to his skivvies and lay down.

The bed in the back of Ray's van was a twin-sized mattress. Once Stevie got settled into it, he looked up to me and said, "You getting in or what?"

I got undressed and got in too. To be honest, I didn't know what to expect. From the time Stevie had gotten into the van with me, I'd felt a huge weight had been lifted away; I felt safe. Both Squirrel and I worshipped the ground that Stevie walked on. As I lay close by him, I waited for him to initiate something. He put his arm around me and nothing happened.

Finally I said, "Hey, Stevie?"

"Yeah?"

"You can fuck me if you want. I know where Ray keeps the Vaseline."

I heard Stevie inhale deeply. The silence seemed to last a full ten seconds.

"Just go to sleep, Kev."

I guess it shows how confused I was–not about my sexual orientation–but about what a real relationship should look like. Thank God, Stevie did the right thing that night. Nothing. I could have felt rejected, but I didn't. He was staying safe with me to keep me safe. I thought I needed to do something in return to pay for his kindness, but all he wanted was to know that Ray wasn't putting me in danger. His arm around me was all I could have asked for that night.

It certainly was what I needed.

The Hat

Despite the horrible reality of being a hustler, Squirrel still managed to be kind and gentle; there wasn't a mean bone in his body. Stevie was also mostly good, only showing violence when someone threatened him or us. That makes one particular incident stand out in my memory. It happened later that summer.

It was one of those hot July days when the sun was blazing and the humidity was oppressive in Tower Grove Park. Early in the day, Stevie decided to run down to a corner store to buy a pack of cigarettes. Before doing so, he asked Squirrel for a special favor: to hold on to his knife.

I was shocked, since I hadn't known that Stevie carried a weapon. Yet considering what we did and where we did it, it wasn't a bad idea.

After Stevie got back we decided to hitch down to Ted Drewes Frozen Custard in southwest St. Louis, all of us forgetting that Squirrel had Stevie's knife. In those days, hitching wasn't hard to do.

When we got to Ted Drewes, Squirrel and I got chocolate custard, and Stevie ordered vanilla. It was my first time visiting the custard stand, and it was amazing. We each ordered our frozen custard. Squirrel and I got chocolate, and Stevie ordered vanilla. When they served us our treats through the window, they first turned the whole concoction upside down in the cup. I guess this was to impress the customer—to add a dramatic flair, to show how firm and concrete the custard was. You couldn't drink it through a straw; you had to eat it with a spoon.

We finished our treats and began walking back to the Tower Grove area. One of us put up a thumb to hitch a ride. Soon enough a car pulled up and we all piled in. Stevie had Squirrel and me sit in the backseat while he rode up front next to the driver. The driver was a middle-aged man driving what seemed like a nice enough car. Despite the fact that the car had air conditioning, the man appeared nervous and sweaty. I knew that if I noticed this, Stevie must have noticed it as well.

"Where you kids heading?"

Stevie answered, "If you could drop us off near Tower Grove, that would be great."

The man didn't respond with a yes or no, only with silence. I looked at Stevie, trying to read him.

The guy broke his silence. "You boys want to have some fun?"

This immediately made all three of us put up our defenses, because we all knew what he meant by fun. He wanted *us*.

"No thanks," Stevie said. "Just drop us off near the park."

About halfway there, the man turned off on a street away from Chippewa, a street going in the opposite direction. Danger bells went off in my head. I knew we were in trouble. Stevie and Squirrel knew it too. Stevie began to reach for something.

A look of horror crossed Squirrel's face. Without saying a word, he pulled out the knife from one of the large pockets in his army jacket. He opened the lock blade, reached around the guy's head, and held the very large and very threatening weapon to the throat of the man who was taking us somewhere we didn't want to go.

I froze.

What struck me the most was the look on Squirrel's face. It was an expression of fear and anger, but sadness too. This wasn't something that the Squirrel I knew wanted to do. Stevie knew it as well.

All Stevie said was, "Do you want to let us out now?"

The man immediately pulled the car over. All three of us piled out of the car as it sped off. None of us said a word as we began walking back toward the park. Stevie took the knife away from Squirrel's trembling hands.

"I'm sorry, buddy," Stevie said. "I'm sorry you had to do that."

Walking next to Squirrel, I noticed that he was crying, and that made me cry too.

Squirrel was a street kid, but the thought of hurting someone, even someone who meant him harm, was repugnant to him. These violent situations were too much for kids like us, but somehow we had to manage.

"It's OK, Squirrel," Stevie said. "I won't let that happen ever again."

When Stevie said that, I knew he meant it. All he ever wanted was to protect us.

AUGUST OF '75 CAME with a rash of Midwest thunderstorms. I remember this, because as kids who lived pretty much outdoors, any rain was inconvenient. Thunderstorms were a downright pain. Not only did we have to seek shelter, but we also had no quick customers in the park. No quick customers meant Ray would be looking to find us dates. By this time, I had gotten to despise Ray. The only reason I kept any contact with him is that, in my childhood mind, I had no other option. If I wanted to be with Stevie and Squirrel, Ray was my only ticket, my only ride.

The next weekend, the three of us walked through a steady rain to eat at a place down near Scanlan and Ivanhoe Avenues called Mother's Pizza; Stevie knew one of the kids who worked in the kitchen. While we were there, the owner, Chuck, struck up a conversation with Stevie. He told us he was getting ready to open a new place on Sydney Street.

"Oh yeah?" Stevie said. "Are you going to call that place Mother's Pizza too?"

"No, I'm going to call it *The Other Mother*."

I thought that was funny. I giggled and the owner glanced at me, smiling.

"I've got a job there for you if you want it, Stevie."

Chuck looked at Stevie, waiting for an answer. I remember seeing his knowing eyes. They were pleading. They were saying, *Hey, kid … You've got other options here.*

"Thanks, Chuck," Stevie said. He looked down at his feet. An uncomfortable pause crept in and hung in the air. Then he added, "Yeah … I'll … I'll keep that in mind."

When the guy walked away, Stevie rolled his eyes and shook his head.

I looked at him and asked, "What?"

Squirrel snickered a little and stood closer to me.

Again I asked, "What?"

All Stevie said was, "Nothing, it's just … he's a nice guy."

Looking back, I realize that there are good people everywhere. Chuck was one of the best. He only had the purest of intentions in reaching out. He only wanted to help. Really help. I still feel a smile sneak to my mouth when I think about him.

Stevie went out the front door, off to the side of the restaurant, to talk with a couple of guys around his age or older. Afterward, he came over to Squirrel and me.

"You guys want to go to a party?" he asked.

Squirrel and I both agreed, and probably for the same reason: it was better than hustling at the park. As we headed out, I noticed that the rain had stopped and little mud puddles littered the street.

WHEN WE GOT to the party, the first thing I noticed besides the smell of cigarette and pot smoke, and the stench of stale beer soaked in the shag carpet, was that everybody was older than me. I'm sure that some were Squirrel and Stevie's age, but we were definitely the kids of the bunch. And I was the *youngest* kid there.

I looked at Squirrel and saw that he was squirming. His eyes scanned the room for danger. The two of us grabbed a beer, found a seat, and tried to make ourselves smaller, unnoticed.

From where I was sitting, I could see into the kitchen. My eyes locked on a guy leaning on a counter. It was Ray. He was talking to another guy around his age. I probably would have just noticed this without giving it much thought. But then Ray pointed me out to the man he was talking with, his finger reaching out almost to touch me from across the room. My stomach felt like it was just dropped off a high cliff—the feeling you get when you're being threatened with real danger.

At about that same time, Stevie materialized out of nowhere and said to us, "Come on, guys, we're getting out of here."

Squirrel immediately said, "Why? I just got this beer."

"Come on, Squirrel. There are some guys here who want a piece of Kev." The high cliff my stomach had fallen off of got taller.

Squirrel furrowed his eyebrows and tilted his head.

"Squirrel," Stevie reiterated. "We have to go. Now!"

"All right, Stevie. Come on, Kevin, let's go." Squirrel grabbed my hand, pulling me off the beer-stained couch. We walked out the front door behind Stevie.

I wasn't exactly sure what was going on, but I got the message that I was the one in danger and Stevie was protecting me, like always. As we walked outside, it started to rain again. It wasn't raining hard, but enough so that we wanted to get out of it.

"Hey guys," Stevie said, "let's go get some beer. I've got a little cash. We're not too far. Follow me."

Stevie led us down two streets, and the rain picked up its pace. We started running.

"Wait up!" Squirrel was falling behind. I stayed with him.

We arrived at the liquor store panting. It was another one where Stevie—most of the time—could pass as old enough to buy whatever he thought he needed. A neon Busch Beer sign glowed bright blue and white in the window. Steve shepherded us toward the door, but Squirrel hesitated. "I'm just going to stay outside," he said.

"What do you mean?" I asked. "It's raining."

"It's OK. I'll just go around the side. There's cover around there."

Stevie shook his head and entered the store. I stood there for a moment, wondering what to do. Squirrel gestured with his hands, shooing me away.

I didn't want to leave Squirrel, but it was raining and I was wet and a little cold. I decided nothing much could happen out in the rain to Squirrel; we'd only be gone a few moments, anyway.

When we stepped back outside, Stevie asked, "Where's Squirrel?"

"Remember? He stayed outside."

There was a pause until he said, "Kevin! *Fuck!*"

"What?"

"You know ... *You know what he's doing!*"

"What?!" I squeaked out.

Stevie pushed me aside to look around. Squirrel wasn't anywhere to be seen.

"Squirrel! Get out here!" Stevie yelled. He sounded like my dad when he was angry and wanted to talk to me immediately.

As I started to worry, Squirrel wandered around the corner from the back alley and stumbled to us.

"Goddammit, Squirrel!" Both frustration and relief were in Stevie's voice.

I looked at Squirrel and saw his glassy eyes. His breath smelled fruity and of chemicals.

"Um. What's up?" Squirrel asked. I knew what was up, but I guess I wanted confirmation from Stevie.

"He's been wanging!"

"Wanging" is a St. Louis term for huffing or sniffing glue.

Squirrel apparently had a fondness for it. It's not like we didn't do things too. We smoked weed and we drank. Stevie loved his Mad Dog 20/20. But we didn't wang like Squirrel. I hated it when he did and so did Stevie.

"Dammit, Squirrel, you're gonna fry your brain doin' that."

Squirrel swayed side to side. He slowly mumbled, "Yeah. Sorry. I won't do it again."

"Damn straight you won't. Give me your gear." Stevie reached into Squirrel's pockets. Squirrel didn't resist. Stevie grabbed a plastic bag and a little tube of airplane glue, and pitched them inside a nearby trash can.

"Come on, let's get out of here," he said.

As always, we followed him.

STEVIE HIT THE bottle hard and fast that night as we walked through the rain. He led us back to Tower Grove, both of us supporting Squirrel's stumbling gait. Because of our extra "responsibility" it took longer than usual to get to the pavilion.

Earlier, Stevie told us we were going to go to the Courtesy, but since Squirrel was all goofed up on glue, all that had changed. We decided that until he sobered up, we needed to put Squirrel in the gazebo, which was situated across from the pavilion at Tower Grove. We couldn't take him to the Courtesy Diner with us, as he'd inevitably say or do something stupid to get us kicked out. Squirrel was not pleased about being left behind.

"Come on, guys," he said, "I want to go. I'll be good. Promise." He tried to stand up, but the glue was hitting him hard and he fell back down.

"No," Stevie said. "Stay right here in the gazebo, out of trouble. We'll go and bring you back a chocolate shake."

"OK," he said with a chemically induced smile as he leaned back.

It was a relief for us that Squirrel would stay put. We knew that by the time we got back, his head would clear.

The Courtesy Diner was about a mile up the street from the circle in Tower Grove, walking distance as long as it wasn't storming. Luckily, the rain had subsided by the time we left the gazebo. *At least we won't get wet*, I thought.

After walking awhile, Stevie cleared his throat.

"Kevin, why do you come out here?" he asked. "You don't need to be doing this."

I felt uncomfortable by Stevie's sudden seriousness. *Is he rejecting me? Doesn't he know that I come here for them?*

"I really don't mind it," I said. "It's not that bad."

"That's bullshit, Kevin. No one likes this." He shook his head and added, "It's really cool that you give most of what you make to Squirrel and me, but you shouldn't even be out here. You don't belong here."

"Well, what about you?" I asked indignantly. "You don't belong out here either. You're one of the smartest guys I know. You know things. You know the important shit you learn in school. And I know you're not from around here; you don't talk like the rest of us."

Stevie thought about that for a bit.

Then he said, "I don't understand you. I don't have a choice. Besides, somebody's gotta look after Squirrel, but you shouldn't be here!"

"Well, what about that? Why are you and Squirrel out here?"

"Don't change the subject! This isn't about us. We're … well, we're here. And this is what we do. This ain't about me an' Squirrel … it's about you. You shouldn't be here!"

This was starting to make me feel bad, like I was being scolded by my mom or dad. I wasn't sure how to respond. I stopped walking as the tears welled up in my eyes. I said, "You really don't know? It's because of you guys—you and Squirrel. I want to be with you guys. I don't have any other real friends like you. *Real friends* …" I drifted off.

"You have other friends in Florissant," he said, adding, "I know you do. You've talked about them!"

"Not *real friends*, Stevie. Not like you guys."

"What do you mean?" he asked, with a definite Southern twang.

"What I mean is that you guys, you two, know me … you know, you really *know* me. I don't have that anywhere else. Not even at home. Well … especially not there."

I was a fourteen-year-old kid who'd had numerous sexual relations with older men for money; Stevie and Squirrel knew that and they cared for me and protected me. Where else could I find that acceptance? I was a gay kid who'd found his two soul mates. And even though Ray used me, and the pedophiles used and abused me, I felt lucky. That's what it came down to: I was willing to put up with Ray and sell myself just so I could be with two guys who loved me exactly as I was. We were family. They were *my* family.

Stevie shrugged. He wasn't one to admit he'd learned something new, even when I know he did.

Though part of Stevie remains a mystery to me–I still don't even know his full name–the side that mattered connected with me on a level that everyone else around me knew was forbidden and "dirty," something to be eschewed and discarded. When it came to protecting Squirrel and me, Stevie didn't just see us in terms of our identity and our work. I know that when I told Stevie I felt lucky, I saw a brief flash of understanding. Today when I close my eyes to remember him the way I want to, this brief understanding is what I recall.

BOTH STEVIE and I noticed the squad car as we walked past Cleveland High School and the Courtesy Diner came into view: it was parked right outside the restaurant. I stopped in my tracks.

"Fuck!"

Stevie looked at me, glanced toward the black-and-white squad car, and paused for a moment. He sighed. Then he resumed walking toward the diner.

"Where the hell are you going?"

"I'm getting Squirrel his shake. Let's be cool and maybe the cop will leave us alone."

As we approached the diner, we slowed down. It was obvious we were both scared. There was no reason either of us should have been afraid of a police officer—at least in theory—but we knew that there seemed to be an understanding between some of them (the good ones) and us. In the bad cops' perception, we were worthless hustlers who could be treated any way they wanted, and no one would say a thing.

As we got closer to the squad car, I observed that both front windows were down. I also noticed that the officer had left his police hat on the passenger seat. Stevie and I looked at each other and exchanged a smile, which meant, *Wow, that would be too easy*. We kept walking past the car, however, and quietly slipped in the front door of the diner.

We walked to the counter. Immediately, the cop turned and looked directly at us. I saw a look of recognition on his face.

"Get the fuck out of here, you little faggots!"

The other customers sitting in one of the booths turned around. No one spoke up.

The lady behind the counter was normally very kind to us. But this time, the cop trumped her hand.

"I'm sorry, guys," she said.

"It's OK," Stevie said. "We're gone." Stevie's head dropped as he turned to leave.

We exited through the glass doors. Stevie looked at the cop's car, then at me with a big grin.

I knew immediately what to do. Stevie went to the front of the diner and began banging on the window with both fists.

"Hey pig, *FUCK YOU!*" Stevie flipped the cop off with both hands. He wagged his butt back and forth with his middle fingers raised, then skipped back from the window with both of his hands high in the air. I then did an incredibly stupid thing: I walked toward the front of the diner where Stevie could see me, held up the cop's hat, and yelled, "I got it, I got it!"

Stevie saw me. And so did the cop. Stevie looked at me with utter horror.

"*RUN!*"

The cop sprang to action and headed for the front door. Stevie and I ran toward Tower Grove separately.

I darted across the street into a residential neighborhood, behind a row of little houses, and then out the other end into Tower Grove. I ran past some trees and then up the area that looked like a long golf course fairway, which led to the pavilion and restrooms. I couldn't remember the last time I'd run that fast for that long. My lungs burned and my legs ached. I thought for sure I'd have beat Stevie to the pavilion, but when I got there all sweaty and out of breath, he was waiting for me.

I walked to the pavilion, put the hat on my head with a big grin, and approached Stevie, who was standing by the circle.

"Y'all're an idiot! You kiddin' me?"

He mimicked me, repeating, "I got it. I got it." But the fear and anger in us didn't last long. As the adrenaline subsided, we both started to laugh. I was euphoric. I felt ten feet tall. I didn't know what I'd do with the hat and I didn't care. How I wish I could have stopped time right then and there ...

Our laughing ended abruptly as we noticed a car pull into the circle entrance, its tires splashing puddles from the recent rain. We froze until we saw that it was a cop car–*that* cop's car. I was smart this time; I dropped the hat and ran toward the pavilion with Stevie. We hid there in the dark, kneeling in a corner behind a wooden lattice wall. Both of us felt confident that if the cop began to move in our direction, we could head out the back and into the dark where he couldn't find us.

As we watched the cop get out of his car, Stevie and I saw something that made both our hearts stop. It was Squirrel. He had obviously heard the two of us laughing, so he'd started walking toward where we'd been standing in the nearby gazebo. He walked right to where I'd left the cop's hat. We watched Squirrel bend over to pick it up as the cop walked right up to him.

Stevie panicked, muttering under his breath, "No, no, *no, no!*"

I just kept whispering, "Squirrel, Squirrel, Squirrel."

Stevie was behind me. We couldn't see Squirrel's face because he was turned away from us, but he no doubt had that goofy grin on his face as he held out the hat for the cop to take. Squirrel was just being polite.

The cop walked aggressively toward Squirrel, towering over him. Instead of taking the hat and leaving, the cop grabbed Squirrel with his left hand and cocked his right arm back in a fist.

From behind the lattice wall I stood and yelled, "NO!"

Stevie put his hand over my mouth right away. The cop paused for a second; I swear he looked directly at me. Then he began to beat Squirrel with his closed fist. When the first blow hit him, Squirrel dropped the hat, shrieked, and began clutching the front of the cop's shirt with both hands. He screamed, "STEVIE! KEVIN!!" As the successive blows smashed his face, he fell quiet, but the cop just kept beating him. I saw Squirrel's arms fall down to his sides; he'd apparently gone unconscious.

The cop hit him a couple of more times. This time, I tore Stevie's hand away from my mouth and yelled, "Please, stop!"

Everything went quiet then.

The cop dropped Squirrel, who fell to the ground like a rag doll. I heard his head hit the pavement and saw the cop stand there for a second. From where we stood, we could see his chest rising and falling with rage. "I don't ever want to see you little faggots back there again!" he yelled. Then he bent over, picked up his hat, got in his car, and left.

We ran to Squirrel as fast as we could. When we got to him, what we saw was the scariest thing I've ever witnessed. Squirrel's face was a mess of blood. His cheek was laid open, and I thought I saw some of his teeth through it. He seemed barely conscious, and was curled up on his side in the fetal position.

I started sobbing. I sat on the ground with Squirrel's head in my lap and my legs on either side of him. He continued rolling on his side and clutched at my leg. He began coughing a little and spit out a tooth. I looked up at Stevie and forced my words through sobs. "Stevie, we've got to get him to a doctor!"

"Stay here with Squirrel," Stevie said. "I'm gonna call Sam. He's got a car."

I sobbed like a baby, saying over and over, "Please, Squirrel, please be OK, please be OK. Oh, God, help us." My wailing was so immense as it burst out of me that I gasped for air as I prayed and pleaded.

I have no idea how long it took Stevie to come back with Sam and his car: minutes, hours, or decades. But eventually they came. Both Stevie and Sam ran out of the car. Stevie barked at me, "Move!"

Sam was apparently not prepared for what was in front of him. He cried out, "Holy shit ..." But then he focused on his task, lifting Squirrel's feet to help Stevie, who lifted Squirrel by the shoulders. I jumped into the back of the car as they eased him in next to me.

In no time, we were roaring down Kingshighway Boulevard toward Barnes Hospital. We pulled up to the emergency room. Stevie jumped out and ran in to grab a nurse. I sat in the back, with Squirrel's head in my lap. He was moaning and trying to mumble something. I kept trying to talk to him, but I'm sure he couldn't hear me, because his head kept rolling from side to side, as if he were delirious.

Finally, Stevie came out with a nurse, who climbed into the backseat to take a look at Squirrel. She simply said, "Oh dear," jumped back out, and returned immediately with a gurney and an assistant. I climbed out of the car and stood next to the open door. Sam stayed put in the driver's seat and stared out the windshield.

I stood there by the open door of Sam's rusty lime-green Fury III, sobbing like a little kid, which is what I was. Then another nurse came out of the entrance, took one look at me, and asked, "Honey, are you OK?"

I nodded. Then I realized that I was soaked in Squirrel's blood through my abdomen and across my lap. My hands were red too. Stevie came out about that time. When it appeared the nurse was going back into the hospital to get someone, we both jumped back in the car and left.

I was still crying and talking like a kid half my age. "Stevie?"

"What?"

"Is Squirrel going to be all right?"

"Yeah, the nurse said he may have some broken bones in his face, and most likely a concussion, but he should be OK."

"Stevie?"

"What!"

"I need to wash my clothes."

"What? Why?" Stevie looked back at me and said, "Oh shit! Sam, take us to your place. I need to take care of him."

Sam swore, yet turned the car toward his house, taking the turn too hard and squealing his tires through the curve.

Once we got to Sam's, Stevie took me into Sam's bathroom and undressed me.

"You can sit around in your underwear until we're finished washing your clothes," he said. But by the time he got me down to my underwear, it was evident that Squirrel's blood had soaked through and was all over my skin as well.

"Steee-vie! I'm all bloody. Why is there so much blood?! *Stevie!*"

"It's all right. Jus' shut up! I'll wash it up."

With each new revelation of how bloody I was, I would start crying all over again. I sat in Sam's tub, which we had to drain once and fill again because the first time I'd stained the water red, and it freaked me out. Finally, Stevie got me out of the tub and began drying me off. I was still crying until he finally stopped.

He looked me in the eye: "Stop crying, dammit. He's going to be fine."

Then he grabbed me and hugged me. I heard one quick sob of desperation from him.

I said, "OK, Stevie. OK, I'll stop crying, I promise."

Squirrel

The next morning, I got a ride back to my home in Florissant from Ray. As usual, he had his own agenda.

"Yeah man … that really sucks about Squirrel," he said. "I'm sure he'll be OK though. That kid's tough."

I didn't answer. *Whatever, Ray.*

"Aw, don't be sad," he said. "Before you know it, he'll be back at it," he said. He spoke while he drove, his eyes on the road. Ray was in his groove. I bet he could rattle off his lines to me in his sleep. He knew how to handle his assembly line workers, his factory widgets. He needed us. But he needed us to be as compliant as possible so that we could make money for him. He was the boss and he was in control, and I hated him for that.

He continued, "When can you get out here again, Kev?"

Bingo. There it is.

"I dunno. I gotta see what's up this week," I said.

"Well … don't forget to give me a call. I want you to see Squirrel again after he gets better."

"OK." *You're such a dick, Ray.*

Going back to my so-called normal life was a comfort because nothing of what had happened the night before (or at Tower Grove that whole summer) existed at home. The only thing that started to seem a little out of place at home was me. I had the sense that there was something different about me, but I couldn't put my finger on it. I had stopped crying the night before.

A few days after Squirrel was beaten, Mom shook me awake as I slept on the top bunk in the room that my brother and I shared. Her shaking startled me, and I shrank away from her until I realized where I was. I had no idea what I'd been dreaming about, but she noticed that my face was soaked with tears and I had been crying. My brother had been bothered by my crying and had gone to get her.

"Are you OK, Kevvy boy?" she asked.

"Yeah, Mom, I'm OK. I must have been having a nightmare."

"Here. Come up and lay on your tummy. Mom will make it all better."

And she rubbed my back, soothing me until I fell back asleep. It was so comforting to know that I didn't have to explain anything. I suppose that whatever she thought was happening to me was symptomatic of what all boys endure in their junior high school years. We didn't talk about it any more. I know she never knew.

Of course, my dad didn't either.

My dad worked a lot. He kept his nose in his own business for the most part. I don't think it was because he didn't care about me. I think it was more that he was interested in providing for his family and making ends meet. He still cared about us and for us. That I knew, because he was always willing to listen to us when any of us kids spoke to him. This whole idea that gay people become gay because of the inattention of their fathers and their overbearing mothers is just nonsense.

In any event, I bear the responsibility for my parents' ignorance into that summer's challenges and difficulties. Like any fourteen-year-old kid who wants his own freedom, I was sneaky. *Unlike* other kids my age, I had gotten so deep into what I was doing that I didn't think I had any other options than to proceed forward, wherever that might take me. The fear I had in being found out made sure of that. I began to get tight lipped about everything. I had the feeling that my parents wondered what was going on with me, but didn't really know what to do about any of it.

There was one conversation that stands out, that I overheard in my room. My mom and my brother were talking. They must have not known I could hear. My mom was asking about what I was doing in my time away from home, why I seemed so sad. My brother said he didn't know. I suppose, since they didn't sit me down on the couch and ask me point blank what the hell was going on, they only racked it up to normal adolescent discontentment. How little they knew. It's not that they didn't care. They just had no idea about what I was really going through.

IT HAD BEEN two weeks since the attack at Tower Grove. I needed to see Squirrel. Right away. The summer was in its dog days. It was mid-August and the days I spent at home seemed to pass as quickly and easily as a radio station flipping from one song to the next. That doesn't mean it was easy for me. Inside, I was aching. The same thought came to me again and again, like a kid's bicycle wheel with a penny stuck in it—the same point clicks and ticks as the rubber turns on the pavement. The bike makes progress down the street, but you don't notice that. You only hear click … click … click.

I gave up. I finally called Ray.

In the seventies, every home had a phone, but they usually only had one. Ours hung in the kitchen, right next to the light switch. It was an off-white plastic box with a rotary dial. Like most parents in homes with teenagers, my dad had installed a super long cord connecting the receiver to the telephone. Ours must have been twenty-five feet long. It was stretched and worn in several places. Any time I had to make my clandestine calls to Ray (or anyone else), I'd simply dial and pull the cord into the next room. This was nothing out of the ordinary. My brother and sister did it too. So speaking with an adult who used me—but who was my only access to my friends—was never any issue.

I asked Ray how Squirrel was doing. When he reported that Squirrel was out of the hospital and with Stevie again, I was so happy. The next thing I knew, I was yelling into the other room, "Hey, Mom, can I spend a night or two at my friend's house?"

That afternoon, I jumped into Ray's van on the other side of St. Ferdinand Park and headed to Tower Grove.

"Kevin."

"Yeah?"

"Glad I could come pick you up to see your friends."

"Uh. Yeah. Thanks, Ray."

"You know ... they've been missing you. I'm glad I can help out."

Yeah, Ray. I bet you are.

The roads were busy that day. Ray was focused on his driving. He seemed equally focused on reminding me who I was, and what was expected of me.

"There are a couple of guys I want you to see."

"OK. I guess. Nothing too long, I hope." I wanted to hang out as much as I could with Squirrel and Stevie.

When Ray finally dropped me off at Tower Grove, I saw Stevie right away, but didn't recognize the kid standing next to him. Soon enough, I realized it was Squirrel. The hospital had shaved Squirrel's beautiful long hair to his scalp. When the cop dropped him on the ground, he'd gotten a huge gash in the back of his head that required many stitches. It explained why I was so drenched in blood that night. Squirrel also had a row of stitches starting at his upper lip and continuing to above his left eye. The whole left side of his face was swollen and distorted. Looking at Squirrel, I thought I was looking at a cancer patient, or maybe a vandalized work of art. All that beautiful long hair gone. And his eyes. One was sealed shut, stained with blue and green skin. The other–well, it was just empty.

Except for a couple of hours that evening when I was off seeing one of Ray's "friends," I stayed with Stevie and Squirrel. Our system was different that night. Where usually I would sit between Stevie and Squirrel, now Squirrel sat between us. Squirrel made no attempt at hustling. Our buddy system changed too. Whenever

Stevie or I went off with some guy, the other would stay behind and sit with Squirrel. I was earning money to give to Squirrel.

Squirrel was different too. All his happiness was gone. He wouldn't sit close to me like he'd always done before. He also wouldn't look me in the eye. I actually had to sit on Squirrel's right side because his left eye was totally closed and he couldn't see out of it. That day, Squirrel just sat there silently. He didn't want to play or run around or anything.

On the second day, we did get him to walk up to the Courtesy Diner with us. That probably sounds insane, but Stevie and I did it out of a sense of defiance. Before we got there, we checked from a distance to make sure there weren't any cops around. Before Squirrel entered the diner, we made sure the nice employees were working. We were defiant, but we weren't stupid. Not anymore.

It felt like everything that made Squirrel *Squirrel* had been beaten out of him. Squirrel was far away, in another place. I would see *Faraway*, the Andrew Wyeth painting, for the first time shortly after this; it was exactly how Squirrel looked, except in the painting the boy is wearing a coonskin cap. Squirrel wore a backwards St. Louis Cardinals baseball cap. Stevie had bought it for him to cover his shaved head.

I went home after two days, wondering if things would change. I wondered if Squirrel would get his bushy tail and bright eyes back. I wondered if he'd put his arm around mine again. I wondered if I'd smell Pixy Stix and musk and cigarette smoke near my breath again.

When I saw him the next week, Squirrel was still sullen and withdrawn. I was starting to dread that something in him was gone forever. As I caught Stevie staring at our friend, I'm certain he felt it too.

Before I left for home, Stevie said, "Kevin, you need to be here next Thursday around five o'clock."

"Why?"

"I've got a surprise for you guys. You're going to love it …" He drifted off momentarily. "Maybe it'll bring Squirrel back. He'll cheer up."

"What is it?"

"Don't worry about it. Just be here."

I was like a toddler who wants to open his birthday present early. "Come on, Stevie, tell me!"

"All right, but I swear to God Almighty, I'll kick your ass if you tell Squirrel."

"Fair enough. What is it?"

"Have you ever been to the Muny?"

"Yeah, when I was little, my mom and dad took me to see *Oliver*. What are we going to see?"

"The Wizard of Oz."

"Squirrel will love that." I smiled.

The Muny Opera had been in Forest Park forever. It was a huge outdoor theater where they put on a lot of big-time, off-Broadway plays. At the very back of the theater was a grassy area where, if you got there soon enough, you could sit and watch the plays for free. That's what we planned to do.

There'd be no hustling that night. We were just going to be three kids going to see *The Wizard of Oz* at the Muny Opera. Granted, Stevie and I normally would have considered ourselves way too old to go see *The Wizard of Oz*, but Stevie wasn't planning this to be cool. He was planning it to help Squirrel.

THE WAIT FOR Thursday was a killer. I tried to keep myself busy doing chores around the house for Mom and Dad, and meeting with my Florissant friend, Steve. But the wait was still hard. As I looked forward to Squirrel's big surprise, the penny in the bike tire seemed to click slower and slower. I hoped Stevie's gift to him would bring him back.

To get there, of course, I had to deal with Ray. I was worried that he'd be busy and wouldn't be able to take me. Fortunately, Ray was able to pick me up and didn't even make any demands on my time. He did say that he had to take a different route. Not that I cared, but it gave me a different view of the city.

As we passed through traffic, I could see the St. Louis Arch advancing in the distance. Ray had the stereo cranked and the Stones were riffing on love and passion. The air was thick like gravy and the sweat seemed to make it stick to your skin. Some say Dallas or Phoenix heat is hot. I'm sure it is. But St. Louis heat has humidity unlike anywhere I've ever experienced. Ray's dirty van didn't have air conditioning, so the wind of our speed and the passing traffic were all that cooled us. We passed the Laclede's Landing area and the Swisher Licorice Factory. The mix of the sweet-acrid smell of processed licorice and the hops and barley mash odor emanating from the Anheuser-Busch plant rose in the air and swirled around. This smell mixed with the crude mass of people and cars and industry and the life that was Saint Louis, Missouri. The smell washed into Ray's van at sixty miles per hour. I will never forget that smell. It proved to be a marker of that time for me.

I met up with Stevie and Squirrel at Tower Grove. Stevie smiled at me, but Squirrel looked away. I thought to myself, *Just give him time. He'll warm up soon enough.*

"We can try to find a ride," Stevie said.

"OK," I said, "Is Sam going to take us?"

"Nah. We'll just hitch one. Even if we don't catch one, we'll still be in time. It's not that far."

We managed to hitch a ride. On the way, I could see that Squirrel was still at the place he'd gone to since he'd come back from the hospital: *faraway*. He didn't ever ask where we were going; he just sat there quietly, off in another place. The only thing he said on the way to the Muny happened when our ride dropped us off by Barnes Hospital, across the street from Forest Park.

"Am I going back to the hospital?"

Stevie put his hand around his shoulder and said, "No, Squirrel. I have a nice surprise for you."

Squirrel showed no emotion, no change. He said in a small voice, "OK."

We darted across the street into Forest Park, turned around, and saw Squirrel lagging behind, so we grabbed him and hurried him along. As we got closer and approached the entrance of the Muny, it was obvious that Squirrel started to recognize where he was.

"I remember this place. I came here when I was a little kid."

We'd arrived early enough to find a good place on the grass. Judging from the crowd of nice, normal families with young kids in tow, we were way too old for the show. But it was something to do that was nowhere near Tower Grove. And it was something to do for Squirrel. As soon as the show began, Squirrel realized it was *The Wizard of Oz* taking place right in front of him and he began to change. He started to become his old self. He started talking and happily commenting on the show, except when the flying monkeys came out—a time when we all got quiet. I even heard him laugh a few times.

Then Squirrel scooted next to me and put his arm through mine. He whispered in my ear, "Wouldn't it be so cool to be up there, Kevin?"

I've thought about what he said to me just then many times since that night. It makes such good sense to me now. *You're an actor at heart, aren't you, Squirrel?* He was always playing some sort of make-believe, whether it was at the castle at Tower Grove Park or pretending to be blown about by the wind. He was a free spirit full of the love of life.

When he scooted up next to me and put his arm through mine, I thought to myself that everything was going to be OK. At that moment in time, on that summer night at the Muny, everything *was* OK.

THE PLAY CAME to an end. It was time for us to go back. We decided to walk back to Tower Grove because we thought we might stop for something to eat. Squirrel had grown quiet again and began to lag behind. If I had to guess, it had everything to do with leaving the wonderful fantasy at the Muny and going back to the horrible reality at Tower Grove Park.

"Come on, Squirrel. Keep up, would you?" Stevie urged Squirrel on, concerned that we stay together. But Squirrel kept on lagging back. He seemed even more distant now than he had been before we saw *The Wizard of Oz*. I wondered what the two of us could do to snap him out of the place he'd gone to. If a special play couldn't do it, what would?

Stevie and I crossed a normally busy street that was surprisingly very empty. After we got to the other side, we turned and saw Squirrel opposite us, near the curb of the boulevard. I yelled at him to catch up and run across the road. Stevie was impatient for sure, but never to the point that it would bring us into danger.

Squirrel looked at me and smiled, not unlike the very first night I met him.

Then he stepped into the street, right in front of an oncoming van. I never saw it coming. I heard the van brake and its tires squeal. The driver tried to react, but it was too late. The van hit Squirrel, and I watched as his body flew away. Squirrel hit the ground hard and must have slid a hundred feet.

He was gone, just like that.

No more Tower Grove. No more Squirrel.

Stevie

After that, I went to a place where I was on autopilot. My body just did what it needed to do. Who knows, maybe being an underage hustler woke some deep-down instinct to survive, an instinct honed to razor sharpness by all the situations I found myself in.

We didn't stick around. Stevie grabbed me, pulled my shirt, and made me run. Pretty soon, he had run ahead of me. Finally, I couldn't take it any longer.

"Stop! Stevie, stop–please!" I yelled. "We can't leave him there!" I was panting for air, but for some reason I wasn't crying. "We … we have … to go back." He finally stopped.

"Fine, go back then!" He threw up his arms in anger when he said this.

"You're coming too, right?"

"No. You go back. Y'all go back now yourself!" His eyes were wide, crazed. "Let 'em take you to Boonville! I don't care. You're the one who killed him anyhow. Why'd you tell him to cross?!" (Boonville was the Missouri State Reformatory; police and parents would threaten kids with Boonville if they were up to no good. It was a real place and a real threat if you were doing what we were doing in that day.)

I started to cry, but not so much to prevent the anger from coming out: "Fuck you, Stevie! Don't say that. Don't ever say that. It … it wasn't my fault …" I took Stevie by his wrist and pleaded with him, "Please. Come back with me."

Stevie snatched his arm away from me. With his other hand, he slapped me hard across the face.

"Fuck you. Y'all on your own now." Then he ran off, and I was alone.

There was no use trying to run after him. I stood there feeling numb, empty, and alone. Really, really alone. I walked around until I got my bearings. *Where in the hell was I?* I finally found Kingshighway and began walking toward Tower Grove Park. I had no idea what I was going to do when I got there. I didn't even think about going to Sam's. One thing I was sure of: I wanted to stay as far away from Ray and that crowd as I could.

It was getting late and I was starting to panic. I couldn't think of how I was going to get home, back to my other life where shit like this didn't happen. I didn't know addresses or street names, other than the main ones. I was just a kid who got to where he was because others had brought him there.

As I came near Tower Grove, I recognized a street on the right that ran off Kingshighway. It was a divided side street. I knew this street, because Ray had dropped me off at a house there earlier in the summer. It was a house where one of my repeat customers lived. It was easy to get to and after that first time, Ray didn't have to drop me off: I could just walk there.

I walked a block or two and saw the house on the right. It was one of those typical south St. Louis homes made out of brick with a small front porch attached. All the houses in the neighborhood looked the same, but I recognized this house by the crappy grass in the front yard. It seemed this guy didn't give a shit about his landscaping. It must have been at least 1:00 a.m., but I went up and knocked anyway. At first, there was nothing. I knocked again, harder.

"Thomas," I yelled. "Mr. Tom!"

Nobody came to the front door, but I kept banging. I was desperate. Finally a light came on from inside and the door opened a crack. It was dark, but I saw Tom's lips mouth, "Who is it?"

"Tom! It's me, Kevin. Can I get a ride home?"

"Where do you live?"

"Florissant."

He breathed out in disgust, "Get *lost*, kid."

"Please Tom," I said, my desperation breaking through. "I'll … stay with you tonight. You can do whatever you want. No charge. Just take me home in the morning."

Tom stood there on the other side of the door, which was still cracked. It didn't take him long to make a decision.

That night, Tom did whatever he wanted to me—a couple of times in fact—before he fell asleep. I didn't sleep at all. When the sun came up, I finally got out of his bed and put my clothes back on. I stood over him for a while before I nudged him awake.

"Wha–?" he asked. "What's wrong?"

"Take. Me. Home," I said.

He jumped to it and didn't argue. We'd made a deal–it was time for him to honor his side of it.

WHEN I GOT home I didn't cry. I was still in shock. As a kid, I didn't have the capacity to make sense of just how much Squirrel meant to me until he was gone. I wondered: Did he mean to step out into the street right in the path of that van? Had he simply given up hope that his life was of value? Was it really my fault? I'll never know. And in a way, whether it was intentional or accidental, perhaps a result of his blind eye and his head injury, it didn't matter. The truth of it was clear to me: it was the cop who killed him. That cop also killed a part of Stevie and me that night too. The fact that society will never call this cop to accountability for what he did kills a little part of me every time I remember it.

I called Ray about a week later on Wednesday. I wanted to know how Stevie was managing with all that had happened. I have to hand it to Ray–he knew how to play me and capitalize on my need to see my friends.

I sat in my living room, the phone receiver to my ear. I sat in silence a long time even after Ray picked up. Ray kept saying, "Hello? Hello?" but he didn't hang up. He knew it was me. I'm sure.

Eventually, I got enough gumption to speak. "How's Stevie?"

I think I heard him lick his lips.

"I don't know, man," he said. "He's been pretty bummed after what happened." Then he added, "He's been asking about you, wondering when you were gonna be back down here."

Bullshit, Ray.

I know it was a lie. Ray saw what cards he had and played them without any conscience or remorse. He started bargaining with me, because he knew I would want to see Stevie and would do just about anything to get a ride down there.

So I said, "Yeah. OK," like I'd done so many times before.

"Come pick me up on Friday over by the St. Ferdinand pond," I told Ray. "I'll be there around four o'clock."

That Friday, Ray was right on time.

He explained it all to me on the way down. It was something new I had to do for him. I wasn't going to have sex with some old guy this time. "You just have to do it with another kid," Ray said. "The guy just wants to watch."

As usual, Ray would only tell me half the story, and I would end up having to figure out the rest on my own. While he was talking, I didn't completely pay attention to him. I was far away by then too.

We got down to Tower Grove a little before five o'clock. As we started to go around the circle, I found myself looking toward the spot where I first saw Stevie and Squirrel, as if I were going to see them sitting there like nothing ever happened. But no one was there—not Squirrel, of course, but not even Stevie. The place looked abandoned.

"Where's Stevie? I don't see him."

Ray told me that he was probably over on the other side of the pavilion, that I should go over to hang out with him for an hour or two while he went to arrange the date. I shot Ray a look. *I'm not falling for that, you asshole.*

"I swear, Kevin; if he's not there he'll definitely be around here somewhere." I just shook my head and jumped out of the van. I simply didn't care anymore.

I walked toward the back of the pavilion where Ray said Stevie would be. I turned the corner and sure enough, there he was.

Stevie was slumped on the ground with his back against the wall, and as I got closer, I could smell the alcohol on him. He was almost passed-out drunk. I sat down next to him and tried to talk to him, but he could barely mumble. I stayed with my slumped-over friend for probably three hours. He never said a word. The longer I sat, the angrier I got. I wanted to see him and talk about Squirrel; I needed to process what had happened. I wanted Stevie to tell me that it all was going to be OK, or maybe even that Squirrel wasn't really dead. But Stevie was just a kid like me, after all. And he was dealing with things the only way he knew how.

In those hours sitting next to him, it occurred to me that maybe Squirrel meant more to Stevie than he'd even meant to me. I hated to think that Stevie drank himself into a stupor because he couldn't bear the pain that he had failed Squirrel, but it was definitely a possibility.

One of the other park boys stuck his head around the corner of the pavilion. "Hey bud, Ray's out looking for you."

I got up and looked down at Stevie, disgusted. "Well then, Stevie. Fuck you, anyway."

I walked off, got in Ray's van, and said, "Let's go. Just take me home after this one."

I spent the whole trip with my head down looking at the floor. It seemed like we traveled for a good twenty minutes or more. The place where we ended up was an average house in an average suburban neighborhood. Ray knocked on the door; as it opened I saw a man obscured through the screen mesh of the storm door.

Through the mesh I heard a bearish male voice.
"Didja bring him?"

Ray answered, "Yeah, I got him, the one you wanted."

When I saw the man's face, I immediately recognized him as the person Ray had been talking to at the party Stevie, Squirrel, and I had gone to near Mother's Pizza two weeks before ... the party where someone wanted a "piece of me."

The man greeted me, smiling. His eyes were wide and creepy. He wanted to talk, but I wasn't in the mood for conversation. I wanted to get it over with and go home.

I was led to a back bedroom. As I entered, I noticed some things that didn't make me feel any better: there was a large bed with no top sheet; next to the bed, two movie cameras were pointing in different angles. I don't know how nice they were, but they looked expensive to me.

The sheetless bed and the cameras weren't what *really* bothered me though. On the mattress, a kid sat eating a couple of Oreo cookies. He was wearing a pair of cutoffs and a tank top-style shirt. He couldn't have been more than nine or ten years old. It was obvious now what I was there for.

I turned and looked Ray right in the eye. "No," I said. "No, Ray, I'm not doing this. No fucking way. I don't want to be in a movie, and I'm not doing that with a little kid."

Maybe Ray or the man didn't see this kid as being that much younger than me. Physically I wasn't that much more mature than he was, but to me he was a little kid. It was twisted beyond comprehension.

Ray tried his usual bargaining tactics. Stevie was his leverage over me, and he knew it. I kept thinking: *This time there is no way ... no way.* I was ready for Ray and I wasn't backing down. I wondered how he would react, but I knew I could handle him if he got in my face. After all, I had stood up to him before.

What I wasn't ready for was Ray's friend. Before I knew what was happening, he had grabbed the hair on the back of my head and bent me backward, facing him. He held my face so close to his that I could smell the cigarettes on his breath.

"Listen, you little faggot, you're going to do what you're told or I'm going to take you out back and beat the shit out of your little faggot ass!"

So there I was, having to choose between two awful things. I was considering the beating option when I noticed the look on the kid's face. It was a look of fear at the violence that was to come; the look took all the fight out of me.

"I'm sorry, I'm sorry," I said. "I'll do it. I'll do it."

God forgive me, I did it. And that's all I'll ever say about that.

AS I WAS WALKING out the door with Ray, I heard the man say to him, "That was good, Ray. I can use him again."

At least the guy was honest. *Using* me. That's exactly what he was doing with me.

Ray was true to his word and took me home. The ride took forever. The whole time I was thinking that I was done with it all. My soul felt tiny and beaten. When we got back to St. Ferdinand Park, it was dark, but all the field lights were on. Every ball field was occupied with suburban kids and older softball players—people who didn't know Ray, people who didn't turn tricks or make pornos with little kids, people who hadn't lost the one they loved because of a bigot cop. Ray drove to the spot where Tim first introduced me to him back in May.

When we stopped he said, "Well, when will we be seeing you again?"

He said "we."

I sat there for a second. "Go to hell, Ray," I said. "I'm not doing this anymore."

He just looked at me. As he was getting ready to respond, I said, "I swear Ray, if you ever bother me again, I'm going to tell everybody what you do and *who you are*. I don't care if they send me to Boonville."

My statement seemed to stop Ray in his tracks. His face changed. It morphed from fear into something grisly and grotesque. His lips tightened. His eyebrows furled. He gripped the wheel of the van. I got scared and got out, not taking my eyes off him for a second.

As I was getting ready to shut the door, Ray looked over at me. He had relaxed, which depressed me more than scared me. He simply said, "It ain't over, Kevin."

I slammed the car door. Enough to get across my message: *It is over, Ray.* As I began walking, I heard the idling of his van growing ever distant. I resisted the urge to turn around and look to see whether Ray would be gunning the van to run me over. But all I heard was the never-ending idling of the engine. I wondered if it really was all done. I wondered what Ray was plotting then and what he'd do to me tomorrow, and the next day. And the next.

I walked home across the ball fields, but as I did I kept an eye on Ray's van just to make sure that he drove out of the park. I was relieved to be home that evening. I sat down in a living room chair, tilted it back against my mom's sewing table, and watched TV with the family. Don't misunderstand. I was totally wrecked, but I had no idea then how bad it was.

The person who'd jumped out of Ray's van had become a jaded little park hustler. I was caring less and less about my normal life. Maybe it wasn't that I didn't care about it; I just found that I had wandered so far afield that I was now lost, and couldn't find my way back. I thought I would still, somehow, have someone who would look out after me, that I wouldn't feel as much like property, a thing to be hawked around town. I would be calling the shots.

Holy fucking God.

How delusional can a person get?

THAT NEXT FRIDAY at about two in the morning I snuck out of my house to walk around St. Ferdinand Park. It was something I'd begun to do to clear my head. I don't remember the first time I did it, but I remember how peaceful and quiet it was. I didn't make the walk every week, and only when the weather was warm, but I enjoyed the solitude when I did. It was a form of therapy, so to speak. I did it because … it was just me.

I crossed the bridge over Coldwater Creek, and began to walk toward the pond, near the playground. A playground for "normal" kids with "normal" lives. As I walked over the hill and into the parking lot, I noticed a junker-type car with three guys near it. Two were sitting on the hood facing away, looking toward the creek across the field, but one was leaning up against the driver's side door facing my direction. At first he didn't seem to notice me, but then I saw him grab the other two's attention and point in my direction. I thought, for some reason, that I must know them, so I waved and began walking in their direction. When I waved, I thought I heard them laugh. As I got closer, I realized I didn't know any of them. They seemed to be teenagers, but not from around my neighborhood. They seemed more like the south-city type. Rough. Mean.

I walked up to them and said with a smile and subdued laugh, "You guys gonna party?"

"We are now," was the response.

From the very beginning there was a voice, down in me, that kept saying, *You're going to get hurt. You're going to get hurt.*

I ignored that voice.

After being dropped off at strangers' doorsteps by Ray, after screwing guys inside their homes or in the back of Ray's van, I'd developed a pretty good intuition, by fourteen-year-old standards, for knowing if someone wanted to use and abuse me. I knew this was the case as soon as I made contact with these jerks by the junky car.

But I still walked right into it.

At some point, I developed a love-hate relationship with death on a subconscious level. There was a part of me that was critically wounded and just praying for someone to deliver the final blow. Put me out of my misery. *Maybe this is it*, I thought. Another part of me desperately wanted someone to rescue me from it all. I had come to believe that Stevie and Squirrel would be that for me. But no more.

Right then, I changed my mind. Whatever I thought I might find with the group by the junky car, wasn't worth it. I figured out what those guys wanted to do, and yes—I basically delivered myself to them—but *I CHANGED MY MIND*. Thing is, there I was, right there in front of them. Like a piece of meat thrown out to hungry circus lions.

One guy got in my face and said, "We're going across the field to the creek an' smoke a joint. Come on with us."

"Thanks, but I think I'm gonna go home."

The guy who had done most of the talking so far just shook his head.

"Come on, Kevin … we won't be long."

By then, all three had surrounded me. The leader grabbed me by the arm. As we walked toward the creek, it dawned on me that he had said, *Come on,* **Kevin**.

I hadn't told them my name. *Had I?*

I also noticed that one of the boys, who had red hair, had a knife that he was playing with in a way so I would notice.

I've mentioned being frightened before, but this was enough to shut me down. As soon as I saw the knife, coupled with the unspoken intent exhibited by all three boys, I knew the knife was meant for me. I couldn't talk; I couldn't run. I was just being led, like a lamb, to the sacrificial altar. I knew they were talking and laughing, but I couldn't … I couldn't make out what they were saying; it was only a strange buzzing in my head. I felt ethereal, like I wasn't there.

At some point, I felt I was simply an observer of it all. To say that I was disembodied isn't completely accurate; I think it was more about the struggle in my mind–I was attempting to grasp that it was all really happening to me. It wasn't a dream, and it *was* happening to *me*. They took me to the far side of the field where it was pitch black and secluded, but I could still see everything they did.

They told me to take off my pants. I kept repeating, "I just want to go home. I just want to go home."

The leader didn't respond, but slapped me hard across the face. I barely even flinched and didn't make a sound. I remember thinking: *If a St. Louis cop slapped the shit out of me in the front seat of his unmarked car after me giving him a blow job, this guy can't faze me much.* I did what I was told; I methodically kicked off my shoes, and slid down my pants and underwear in one motion.

I'd done this before. *This is what I do. Right?*

I remember it all. Every detail.

It was full-on gang rape. I'd never had that happen before. It was terrifying, not because they were fucking me, but because all the guys seemed to get off on it so much. It's like I was nothing. Kevin was nothing. He'd diminished into a sack of meat, one that stood there and just took it.

What I will say, and what I have no explanation for, is that during the entire time, I felt as though there was someone else right up next to me who understood what I felt. No, it wasn't a religious experience. It felt like Squirrel. I couldn't see him, but it felt like him. I know it sounds fake, but it's what I felt. As the assault happened, all I focused on was not getting stabbed with that big goddamned knife.

After they had finished with me, I remember seeing myself from a distance, on my knees with my hands raised up in front of me, as if I was about to protect myself from a blow. The boys' discussion began to slowly come back in focus.

"We better go, it's getting too late."

"No. Wait …" the red-haired one said. "Wait, watch this …"

The big guy stood next to me with his knife and said, "Put your hands down."

I kept repeating, "I'm sorry, I'm sorry, I'm sorry …"

"Put your hands down!" another said.

"Put your hands down, ya little faggot!"

They grabbed my wrists and forced them back. I saw the guy with the knife stab me in the chest.

"You're done. Now you're finished," he said. The others laughed.

He killed me. I'd seen the knife go in and come out.

I know that couldn't have happened, but it's what I saw. If they stabbed me—for real—I'd be dead. *Right?*

And that's where it all ended.

I fell face forward and I heard the words reverberate in my head. *You're done. Now you're finished.*

I passed out.

I DON'T KNOW how long I lay in that field, but I woke up naked, except for my socks, alone and sobbing. I felt my chest to see if there was any blood, but it was dry. I didn't exactly understand what the kid with the knife had done. The blade itself looked real enough, so I didn't think it was fake or some kind of trick knife or prop. Maybe the guy holding it flipped it back right when it got to my chest, only pressing his wrist into me. I just didn't know. It was dark, so I guess it was possible he had done that. What I did know was that *I felt the blade enter me.*

I can't explain it. I'm not one to believe in miracles, at least not like this, but maybe someone saved me. Maybe it was Squirrel, who was there in spirit the whole time, who took all the sadism and hatred of those boys into himself, saving me. After it all happened, I do know I passed out. When I woke, I was relieved to be alive.

I managed to stand and get dressed. I snuck back into my house, which was a miracle, considering the state of mind I was in. I went to the bathroom in the hallway. I sat on the toilet for a while, passing everything, trying to get it all out. I flushed, then got down on my knees and began vomiting. After a while, a knock came through the bathroom door; it was my mom.

"Are you OK?"

"Yeah, Mom, just a little sick. I'm fine." Faking it and lying to my mom was automatic, as always.

After I had finished, I walked out to the kitchen. Mom was waiting for me, still in her nightgown. I was drenched in sweat and my mouth was dry.

There was a little ritual I would go through when I had thrown up. Mom would give me a few saltines and a small glass of 7UP. These things were waiting for me when I walked into the kitchen. This little gesture, though it felt surreal, was so very welcome and *normal*. I didn't say a word; I just sat down and ate my saltines and drank my 7UP.

"Kevvy ... really now ... are you sure you're fine?" my mom asked. She had reached around and put her hand on my shoulder. She looked right at me very intently, like all mothers do, I suppose, when they're worried about their child.

I laid my head on her chest and said, "Yep."

I went back to my room, but before I went to bed, I took out the cross that had most of the silver rubbed off it. I removed it from around my neck and put it in a small wooden box. I just left it there. I looked at the ceiling and, feeling numb and vacant, fell asleep.

That was it. That was the end of my summer.

AROUND THE END of October in the lunchroom of Hazelwood Central High, I noticed Tim, the one who had introduced me to Ray earlier that year. He was across the cafeteria, watching me. It looked like he was waiting for my friends to leave. When I noticed this, I left the lunchroom, explaining to my friends that I had to grab something from my locker before the next class. Tim followed me. When I was almost to my locker, he yelled out, "Kevin, wait."

I turned to him. "What the fuck do you want?"

Tim looked sad and pathetic; evidently, he didn't want to be talking with me either.

"I'm supposed to tell you something."

"Tell me what?" I figured he had a message from Ray.

"Stevie's dead. They found him in an empty lot somewhere downtown. Ray said he probably got drunk and froze to death." I believed him. That October had started out quite warm, but in the week leading up to Tim's news it had gotten frigid at night.

Hearing about Stevie's death caught me off guard. I stopped. I just looked at Tim, but he couldn't look back. He stared at the floor.

I said, "Was there … is there … going to be a funeral?"

"Not that I know of," he said.

"Well, where's he buried?"

"I don't know. Nowhere, I guess." And then Tim left.

I stood next to the locker for a long time. It was all over. Really over.

Goodness

I didn't say a word to anyone.

Thinking back on the night with my mom, I know that if I'd just begun crying and spilling the beans to her, she might have embraced me. She might have even gotten me the help *she* thought I needed. But, I didn't know. I was afraid to say anything. In some ways, it's better I kept quiet. To be honest, I don't go there right now. I don't wonder about what *could have* or even what *should have* happened, because I *didn't* tell her anything. And I never will. I have to live with that.

I knew that my parents did wonder though.

I write that, because later, when I had turned fifteen, my dad announced that I was going to see a doctor. The reason he gave me was my feet. That's right, my feet. My toes would dry out and crack all the time, and my parents knew this. At times it was painful, but just like everything else, I was stoic and just put up with it. So when my dad said that I was going to the doctor to have my feet looked at, I didn't think it was too terribly weird, other than the fact that my dad never took us to the doctor, unless it was for stitches or broken bones.

The day came for me to see the doctor. When I was ushered into the back, the nurse told me to take off my clothes and put on a gown. *Why the hell should I put on a gown when all the doc's gotta look at are my feet?* I did what I was told, but having spent the previous summer disrobing countless times for countless men, I felt my blood pressure rise and my heart beat faster. Understand—it was out of fear, not excitement.

The doc came in the room and greeted me. He was a tad overweight and slightly balding, but not too hideous. This is one of the lovely side effects from that summer that seems to have stayed with me to this day: whenever I meet a guy for the first time, I immediately size him up as a potential john. It's really unsettling to me that this reflex is still there. In any case, I got more and more anxious sitting there in my gown in the clinic.

The doctor began giving me a full physical exam, checking my eyes, ears, and reflexes, and my heart. He then had me face him. "Pull down your underwear, please," he said.

Aw fuck, here it comes.

Luckily, it was just the turn-your-head-and-cough routine.

"OK, now turn around and bend over and spread your legs."

Wait. What? FUCK NO! I simply refused. I didn't know what he might find back there, but it scared the hell out of me, knowing what I'd been doing that previous summer. I didn't want anything back there giving my little secret away. So, I just refused. We went back and forth a little while, but after a bit, he dropped it.

"Well … OK," he sighed.

He had me put my robe back on and invited me to sit in a chair next to his desk. He took out a pen and began asking me a series of questions, noting my answers on a piece of paper.

"How are you with your mom and dad?"

"What do you mean?"

"You know. Do you get along?"

"Yeah. I s'pose."

"Do you tell them about what's going on during the day?"

I shrugged and nodded.

"How are you doing in school? Do you have any friends? How close are you to them? Do you get into a lot of fights?" Things like that.

All my answers were short and terse. Yes. No. I don't know. OK, I guess.

The whole time I was frazzled by the fact that he wanted to look at my ass.

The doctor stopped for a second, looked up from the paper, and gave me a smile. "You look really cute in that robe, Kevin," he said. He chuckled.

The thing was, he probably wasn't a bad guy at all. When I look back on it, I realize that he didn't do or say anything inappropriate. Yet the "You look really cute in that robe, Kevin" line made me snap.

"I'm done," I said. I never got violent. I was just done. It was too much for me.

I quickly dressed and walked out to the waiting room where my dad was. I sat down next to him. "Can we go now?"

The doctor followed me out. He didn't seem upset, but asked my dad to come into the room without me. He was in there for only a couple of minutes, but it seemed like hours. When Dad came out he looked pissed. *Aw fuck! He knows.*

"Come on, Kevin," he said. "Let's go."

At first I was scared to ask my dad anything about what the doctor might have said. Finally I mustered up the courage. "What'd the doctor say, Dad?"

"He wanted to put you on some drugs," he said.

The doctor never did look at my feet.

MOST OF MY life, I pretended like none of it occurred. I went back to St. Ferdinand Park throughout high school, but always with friends, which wasn't easy, since I kept everything all to myself. The reality at the time was that boys my age found hustling in a public park weren't seen as victims, but as delinquents. If boys like me were taken anywhere, it was to a juvenile jail facility.

What happened since the summer of '75 has been like living a life of nightmares, both asleep and awake. For a while, I was terrified of crowded and unfamiliar places. I remember going to concerts with my "normal" friends, armed with a big knife hidden under my jacket. I'm still very uncomfortable in crowds unless I'm with someone I know and trust. Sex and relationships have been a huge mess. I spent countless years trying to be straight, and in doing so, accomplished nothing except hurting some wonderful women. Since I was raped at the park that night, I've been unable to have any sense of intimacy or fulfillment in sex. I'm easily distracted. I've long been telling people that I have ADHD. I can be easily startled. A simple tap on the shoulder to get my attention can make me jump out of my skin.

It doesn't take a psychologist to guess I've been carrying around a serious case of PTSD for all these years. I know that now, but I didn't attach myself to that idea until recently, after I started seeing a therapist. For some reason, I just assumed PTSD was a condition that only afflicted veterans returning from war. The fact that I had been living with PTSD didn't sink in until I was diagnosed with such. It was a very strange moment for me; everything that had happened to me became real once again. In a way, it's good having a name to connect to your state of mind, but I have to admit that I do envy those guys who've been damaged on the battlefield. When they came home they received medals and respect, mostly. There's no shame in telling the world about what they're dealing with, and they have others they can share their experiences with.

With me, sometimes I think I'm the only survivor. No parades, no medals, no comrades, just me. Since I've written the whole thing down, I understand this isn't true. I hope someone else reads my story and can relate. I hope someone else will come forward and say, "It happened to me too."

LIKE I WROTE in the opening chapters, I didn't kill myself. I'm still here. I choose to believe that I'm here for a reason. As I began to process the summer of '75 and what it all meant, I started to realize that it was a story others were interested in knowing about. Not only have LGBTQ rights in the United States progressed to a point I never dreamed of (I wrote much of my story in 2013-14, a game-changing time for us), but also the issue of human trafficking has entered into the public's awareness like never before. However, no writer has yet touched upon *the human trafficking of boys*. I found the reason to tell our story.

SO HERE I am, thirty-nine years later. For a good while I thought I'd buried it all, but like any self-respecting zombie, the story would come out of its grave from time to time and walk around. The truth, unfortunately, is that I never forgot. That summer has shaded every second of my life since then. I know that must sound pretty grim, and it's been hard, but I'm still here; I am alive, and that's important. I am a survivor of one of society's dirty little secrets. I know there must be more of us out there. I think (I don't know for sure) that I was different from most of the kids hustling at the park. So many of those kids lived that life because they needed the money to survive, and that was the easiest way for them to make a buck. But I did it for a completely different reason–for real friendship. I would gather that the majority of the others were gay, but not all.

As I mentioned in the story, I never knew Squirrel's real name. Several times I thought to see if I could look up an obituary to fill in more of the details of his death. The fact that he and his mother could have been homeless makes the idea of following through with this idea all that more difficult–I don't think I'd be able to find anything on them. It would also be emotional torture for me to see his name in an obituary. I want to remember him for who he was for me. Some things are just best left alone, I figure.

Stevie was never forthcoming with his situation. My guess is that he was a *pushout* kid–his family found out he was gay and they kicked him out. Honestly, though, it doesn't matter much. Even though I didn't know the details of where they came from, or even their full names, I know that I *really* knew Stevie and Squirrel. Our friendships had depth because of the place we found ourselves in.

Of course, I was out hustling for another reason: a charming predator used and manipulated me. Before Ray took me to Tower Grove, I didn't see myself as a hustler. I was a naive kid, and I thought Ray liked me and saw me as a friend. I wanted to be around him. Yes, he would give me a few bucks after we had sex, but I interpreted that as a form of affection. It wasn't until after a man two and a half times older than me handed over an envelope full of money that it hit me. I probably would have ended it all after that night, had I not met Stevie and Squirrel.

THERE'S NO DOUBT I was a dumb fourteen-year-old kid, but I had no illusions as to my sexuality, and what that meant in that day and age. Even though I knew that Mom and Dad loved me, it was crystal clear, at least to my fourteen-year-old brain, how they felt about homosexuals. It's not as if they sat me down one day and told me exactly what they thought of them, but then they didn't have to. A kid hears the message, clearly, as a by-product of conversations with the friends your parents have over, or the jokes you heard, and especially the words that are used to describe us–*to describe me*. If the subject was mentioned on TV or in the news, it was about gay men being arrested. In 1975, by the time a gay kid was fourteen, he knew in no uncertain terms who he was, what he was, and that being gay was not only wrong, but also illegal. Not to mention worthy of damnation.

I knew I wasn't going to change, so I slowly got used to being different, an outcast. When society, the church, and your own family devalue you, you devalue yourself. When a kid buys that lie, it's not that far of a leap to allow oneself to be treated horribly. I suppose one of the reasons I could deal with being sold was that the world said we were not worth anything to begin with. We could be bought and sold, beaten and killed, and that was allowed. As I watched the cop beat Squirrel half to death, there was no fear in him; that is, he did it out in the open, as if he didn't care who saw him. He knew he wouldn't get in trouble.

I remember a little incident that happened in my neighborhood a couple of years after that summer, an incident I haven't mentioned yet. Two women moved into a house just a couple of houses down from us. It was common knowledge that those two were a couple. I remember this clearly, because I was waiting to see how the neighborhood would react. I actually allowed myself to get hopeful, until one evening when a neighborhood kid and some of his friends threw some gasoline on the outside of their house and tried to set it on fire. They set the fire poorly, thank God, and it was out even before the fire department responded. I remember seeing the police at their house shortly after.

The usual procedure, even then, would be for the cops to start knocking on doors and asking neighbors if they had seen anything. That didn't happen. It was like it wasn't even worthy of an investigation. I mean, I understood what the score was, but that incident reinforced the idea that it was OK to try and kill *us*, because there would be no consequences. By that time it was the late seventies. That's not that long ago, and shit like that and worse happened.

So Stevie, Squirrel, and I bought "the big" lie, as I am sure thousands of us did. We lived in a dark, lonely world. We knew this, but you need to know that Stevie, Squirrel, and I weren't there out of our own volition. Evil people and an evil culture of hate and neglect placed us there. We knew what we were doing wasn't good, and we were told in no uncertain terms that this was so. But I saw ever so slightly then, and quite clearly now, a reality that no one else, even us, seemed to notice was at work. What I saw was goodness both in Stevie and Squirrel, and yes, even in myself.

If you read and understand nothing else from my story, know this: Squirrel was a *Holy Martyr* and Stevie was a *Holy Saint*. Some might think that what they did precludes the tags *Martyr* or *Saint*, but that's exactly what they were for me. Goodness ran through their blood. And their blood, spilled, has affected me deeply in the sense of justice I have.

There was a kindness and gentleness in Squirrel that I had never seen before. In spite of what must have been a horrible past for him, I experienced a wonderful lightness in him that I don't often see. Until his last days his joy and imagination drew me to him like no other. Squirrel and I would laugh all the time. In fact, that summer gave me just as many good memories as bad, maybe even more good ones. He could imitate just about anyone and make you laugh. I imagine he would have become a talented actor, had he been given the chance. I experienced with Squirrel the most genuine intimacy that I ever had, and I am not talking about sex. He would sit up close to me with his arm hooked in mine; he was my true friend, my lover. We were jaded, tough kids, but there was nothing threatening about him.

Even though I lost him, I will thank God to the end of my days that I knew him, for even a little bit.

Stevie would have become a good, good man.

He looked out for us and let us know that—at least to him—we had value. Coming from Stevie, that meant a lot. He was incredibly smart and caring. Although, like the rest of us, he was terribly, terribly wounded.

I know my last words to Stevie were awful, and I pray to God that he didn't hear, but I hope he now knows how much of a difference he made in my life. To me, he was what it meant to be cool, what it meant to be a man. He was a mature presence of respect and our mighty fortress in times of trouble. In my life, I strive everyday to be the man who I knew he would have become, the man he was. I know that Stevie's response to me after the van slammed into Squirrel wasn't because he really blamed *me*. He said those harsh words to me because in his world, when bad things happened, you needed someone to blame. I was the only one there. In my mind that's what makes him even more of a saint—he was only human, with faults just like me. I forgave him long ago for any blame I felt in Squirrel's death. I remember him today for all he did for us.

And me—well, as harsh a self-critic as I am, I guess I have to admit I haven't done half-bad. I lived and I became a pastor. I've served congregations and cared for people, first in Kansas, then Hawaii. My theology was forged that summer, though I certainly didn't know it then.

ABOUT TWENTY-FIVE years ago, I was in a church not long after Easter. The lector read from the twentieth chapter of the Gospel of John. I heard the story of how Jesus had appeared to the disciples, and they were telling Thomas all about it, but he wouldn't believe. *"But he said to them, 'Unless I see the mark of the nails in his hands, and put my finger in the mark of the nails and my hand in his side, I will not believe.'"*

Yes. I totally get that.

Thomas was traumatized; he was pissed off and had no room for celebration. He had seen someone he loved and trusted brutally murdered in the most shameful way, crucified like a criminal. He naturally couldn't believe. I'm there, man. I get that struggle.

When Jesus appeared to Thomas, he did so with horrible wounds all over his body. I believe firmly that God remained wounded, and God continues to remain wounded. It's the wounded God that makes a difference to wounded people.

And that's what I want to tell Stevie and Squirrel: the three of us *do* have a God, and it is the only God that we can believe in. If Christ had come out of the tomb without a scratch, I wouldn't believe. At least for me, and, as far as I can see, for Stevie and Squirrel, that's the difference between life and death. Stevie, Squirrel, and I were horribly wounded and damaged, and yet we were good kids. What's more is that there are others like us. Thousands of others bought and sold and shoved aside. We're all wounded. I believe that I have a God who is wounded too. For me, it's what's carried me through this whole thing and brought me where I am today.

I want the world to know that once there lived two boys who were good and valued. I want the world to know that Stevie and Squirrel lived. I honestly don't think Stevie ever had a funeral, nor even a grave. Squirrel, I would imagine, did, but I just don't know. One day I fully intend to hold that service for both of them, but before I do, I want people to know who they were. I think when enough people know that these guys lived and died, when more people know how much we have wept for what has been lost, then we will have that funeral.

I'm done with mourning alone.

Stevie and Squirrel: I love you guys; I always will.

Hope

The island of Oahu is a complex mix of a modern American city, a Polynesian island with beautiful views, various strategically placed military bases, miles and miles of white sand beaches open to every surfer and vacationer, and a culture that is part of the United States, but nicely set apart from the influence of the mainland. I've lived there several years now, and though it has no doubt lost the novelty it once had for me, I still notice how beautiful and unique it is every day.

Oahu is approximately 3,700 miles from St. Louis. I suppose it was an unconscious decision to move as far away from St. Louis as I could. Maybe I thought that if I were far enough away, that summer would fade enough in my memory so that I could begin to live normally. But you can probably guess this wasn't the case. Where I go, my memories come too. When you bury something like that deeper inside yourself, it only fights to make itself more known.

I live in Kaneohe, opposite of Honolulu on Oahu's eastern shore. The volcanic hills surrounding my condo rise into the clouds like pillars supporting the blue sky above. I'm fortunate where I live; directly out two sliding glass doors of my condo, a raised lanai, or open veranda, sits above a private space below. The view from the lanai is spectacular. I can see the bay–only a block away–which is an ancient basin of the magma cone of the volcano that formed the island. Directly beyond my porch sits an open green field of grass. That's pretty rare. You don't see that much since developers covet whatever open space they can get to build on. Beyond the field is a path where I like to jog.

I like living in Hawaii, and I'm good at the work that brought me here. I'm an ordained minister—which I know that Squirrel (and especially Stevie) would find hysterical. Today I know the road I took was the right one.

WHEN I WAS thirty-two, I walked into a Lutheran church in Hazelwood, Missouri. It was a church that I remember seeing from the bus, on my way to school. I had just quit my job at a residential center for emotionally disturbed children and adolescents, where I'd been for several years after receiving a BA in psychology. I had become burned out and had a series of jobs after that, from selling retail electronics to bartending to driving a horse and carriage in the city. The morning I walked into the church I was in an existential funk, wondering where my life was headed.

I've always enjoyed the liturgy and the music in worship. There is a side of me that has always been drawn to theater and drama. That morning I was really digging it. After the service was done, the associate pastor spotted me sitting by myself in a pew. His name was Paul. He was about my age and did a pretty good job of making me feel welcome. He wasn't intrusive, just welcoming. Before I knew it, I had joined the church and became more involved.

At that time, I was still looking for some decent employment, and I finally got a heads-up about a job opening up at the local Ford assembly plant. It would have been a steady union job with benefits. Pastor Paul caught wind of this and for some reason objected to this career path for me. He asked me if I had ever thought about becoming a pastor, to which I responded, "No way!"

He disagreed with my self-assessment, and began bugging me to go to Wartburg Seminary in Dubuque, Iowa, for a weekend just to check it out. Finally, just to get him off my back, I registered for an "exploratory" weekend. Now here I am, almost twenty years later, in ordained ministry. Today, I know I'm in the right field. Why? It has to do with my worldview. The idea of a God who would give it all up to be one of us, and then give the finger to the rich and powerful while hanging with thieves, beggars—and prostitutes—seemed to make a lot of sense to me. I'm not in anyone's face with my faith. I want only to be there for others, to care, and to make a difference in the world.

I FIRST TOOK a call (a job) leading a church in Salina, Kansas. Eventually, I took one in Hawaii. I care about the people in my parish and I strive to know their lives, even though they occasionally annoy me with their pettiness. I preach a decent sermon passing on the Good News, and I sing in a community choir. It's a great place and a coveted call; there aren't many Lutheran churches in Hawaii. To be where I'm at is a gift. Nonetheless, I know that one of the reasons I pursued a job at my church was to get away from my past. Unless I went to Antarctica, I don't think I could get any farther away from St. Louis and Tower Grove Park than where I am now.

Thing is, I haven't gotten away from it. It still followed me. Not long ago, I finally had enough of the sleepless nights and constant fear of both people and situations that put me on edge. When a trauma wears a deep enough path in a person's psyche, it just becomes an everyday part of you. But it's an unbearable thing and not especially conducive to functioning well in life. You begin to wonder if the only way the trauma will go away is if *you* go away. So I decided to do something about it, before it did any more to me. Thank God, I finally decided to see a psychologist in Honolulu.

Our weekly sessions have helped me dig up the past and process it. I've gotten healthier as a result. What I experienced in the summer of 1975 has lost its raw power, although it's still there. Part of the experience's power came from its secret nature. No one knew what had happened that summer except me. Now, writing about it and talking about it with others has helped diffuse the power it had over me. Talking isn't just talking, either. It's about revealing. Revealing difficult truths to another helps destroy the grip of shame. I think this is something we've lost in our culture. We think that talking can't *do* anything, but I believe it does. Of course, I'm biased; part of my job as a pastor requires lots of listening. Maybe it's anecdotal, but I observe that it makes a difference all the time. That doesn't mean that talking about our most painful wounds isn't hard. It is extremely difficult.

Despite my background—or perhaps in part because of it—I am a good pastor. I'm a solid theologian and great speaker. Most importantly, I love my people; I care about their lives. I don't necessarily fit the expectation of how a pastor should look or act, with my tattoos, hipster clothing, and punk style, but I believe that's a good thing. For too long, the church has been steeped in moralistic thinking instead of being about radical grace and unconditional love, like I first saw in Stevie and Squirrel. My unconventional character is my asset—it helps convey the radical grace to those outside of society.

One of the central beliefs of the Christian faith is that God meets us where we're at, not where we think we're expected to be. This is the heart of incarnational theology, the belief that God isn't some ethereal being, light-years away, but right here with us in the everyday: the dirt, the joy, the pain, and the mundane. I believe I've been called to tell my story not because I relish wallowing in my own pain, but because others may see that their pain is shared.

My past isn't the totality of who I am, but it did happen. If I can make some good come of it, challenge the world to see Stevie and Squirrel and the thousands of other boys like them as redeemable, then it will help heal my pain and theirs.

There's much healing work to be done on my end. I still find it hard to enter another person's home. That's a challenge when you're a pastor; it's part of my job to enter into people's private lives, including visiting them in their homes. But I'm getting there. After many years of hiding an open wound, I feel as if I have begun to heal. As terrible as that summer was, I understand now that I would have been far worse off had I not known Stevie and Squirrel.

HOW COULD YOU? I have heard these words in my mind and have seen the look on people's faces when I have tried to tell them about the summer of my fourteenth year. As an ELCA minister serving in Hawaii, I wonder how people will receive this book. The fear builds and turns into a voice in my head: *How could you allow yourself to be used by so many? How could you allow yourself to be bought and sold like that? How could you do those things with those men at such an age? How could you?*

I have an easy answer …

It was you. You, my city. You, my schools. Yes, you, my church. And yes, even you, my friends. And though you never dreamed of hurting me—you, my family. You made it clear to each and every single one of us in no uncertain terms what we were worth. God forgive us, we believed you. When every message you get from your society, school, church, and even family and friends on the subject of homosexuality is one of utter damnation and complete worthlessness, it becomes surprisingly easy to sell yourself. Because you see, at least then, you're worth something to somebody. When you are told you are worthy of nothing but hell, you begin to not care about whether or not what you are doing is against the law, or whether it conforms to what society thinks is proper. All you care about is finding someone who accepts you just as you are.

I CAN TELL you this: not one of us gay kids hustling in that park would have ever dreamt of hurting someone in the manner in which people hurt us, in the manner in which my friend Squirrel was treated.

We were just kids.

Stevie, Squirrel, and I: we were kids. We were good kids. I have never found truer friends before or since.

So now I ask you, my city, my schools, my church, my society: *How could **you** let this happen?* Were we gay kids so dangerous, such a threat, such a stain that we could be buried and forgotten? I hold no one person liable, but a system of many individuals, who together gave a nod and a thumbs-up to the active discrimination we experienced.

I know this sounds angry. It is. There's been a load of injustice in the world toward us. Please understand this is the anger of a fourteen-year-old kid. Today I've transformed that anger into action. I know that people can and do change. And I know there are allies everywhere. I'm still hopeful. If I didn't have hope, I wouldn't have written my story.

People have asked me: *Where is the hope in what happened to you, or what was your redemption?* Oftentimes you may hear a pastor who is in the midst of a tragedy or a horrible scene proclaim that he is seeking the grace in all of it. I have spent over thirty-seven years just avoiding any stray thought or recollection of that summer; in the process, I also ended up banishing the thoughts and memories of those who were so dear to me.

But it's a fair question: *Where is the redemption?*

For me, that's easy: it's that I'm still here. I'm alive and I'm writing this today to tell my story in the hope that it will bring awareness to the evils of prostitution, and that there is hope beyond all of the shit to make a real life for yourself. It would have been easier for me to do this, had I not lived in a culture that turned its eyes away from the problems out there for us boys. Still, I made it. And I made a difference to others, not only in writing my story, but also in what I have given to another kid.

BACK IN 2000, when I was in seminary, I took in a kid named Scott. I had taken care of him off and on from the time he was about fourteen, owing to his mother's drug addiction. When he was seventeen, he and his younger brother and sister were finally removed from his mother's custody. The two younger ones were placed with family who could care for them, since they were younger and more manageable. Scott, on the other hand, made it clear that he would not be living with those family members and would instead move back to Vancouver, British Columbia, and basically couch surf. I was contacted by his family and asked if I would consider taking Scotty in. I told them that it really didn't matter what I would consider unless Scott made it clear to me that this was something that he could live with. He agreed. So there I found myself, a first-call pastor (in the parish immediately after seminary education) receiving a call to a church in central Kansas so I could be with Scotty, who was just this side of a street thug and entering his senior year in high school.

As I write this, Scotty's mom is presently visiting us here in Hawaii. She has been five years clean and is actively working on repairing things not just with Scotty, but also with all her children.

And Scotty?

Well, he graduated from the University of Hawaii summa cum laude with a degree in marketing and is presently running a business in Honolulu. Also, as I write this, the states of Minnesota and Hawaii have just made it legal for same-sex couples to be married. It's all happened so quickly. In fact, in Minnesota not just six months prior, an anti-gay group led a battle to enshrine a constitutional amendment to ban gay marriage forever in that state. They failed. Now, states are winning the battle in courtrooms. I continue to hope that one day, worldwide, people will not see gay people as an aberration, a biological error to correct, but as whole human beings who have worth and value in the world. But the challenge remains. Many other countries, especially in Africa, have been emboldened by their hatred against LGBTQ people. So our work isn't finished. Not by any means.

Hope and redemption are always works in progress, but when you ask me about my hope and my redemption, I will point

to my son, Scotty, whom I raised, and who is making it, despite
the odds. (Scott is heterosexual, by the way. I mention this only
to put another misinformed stereotype to rest.) I will also point to
his mom, who continues to get better, and I will even point to the
progress that is being made in our state legislatures. One of the
hardest things for me in this whole ordeal has been the loneliness
of dealing with it all on my own. I know there are others like me
out there. To them, I'll say this: Dudes, maybe it's time that we
come in from the cold. We don't have to do this alone. I'm here.
And there are allies everywhere.

And I continue to believe and to hope. It's the hope that
others will look at us not as the other, the different, but as human
beings. I keep telling myself that one day we will make it.

THIRTY-SEVEN YEARS after that summer, I was going through some
of my old stuff I kept hidden in a trunk, stuffed far back in a corner
of my closet in my home in Hawaii. Digging through the various
letters and old pictures, I came across a plain, old cross that had
most of the silver rubbed off it. It looked pretty much like it did
that night I took it off from around my neck.

I embraced the worn cross in my hand; the chain was still
in one piece, with the cross attached to it. I wrapped my fingers
around the bundle of metal, and I could feel the memories of that
summer in that little pile of silver. The chain was light, but the
memories were heavy, and a wave of loss and fear flowed through
me. I went to my bed and sat down on the corner of the mattress. I
looked up at the wall behind my bed, where I'd hung the painting
of the boy in the coonskin cap. I felt the bottom of my eyes seep,
and my vision went blurry.

If only I hadn't taken that damn cop's hat that day. If only I
wouldn't have urged Squirrel to cross that street. I know it wasn't
my fault, ultimately. I know that bad things just happen, but the
feeling of helplessness nearly forty years after it all went down

was tough. The pain went down deep. The knot in my gut pulled me out of myself and I lost control. I sobbed, gasping for air as my face crunched into a ball of despair and the tears flowed down my cheeks.

I sat on the corner of my bed for a while. The sorrow passed. Looking at the picture again, the little kid stared once again beyond me, *faraway*. And then I realized something—I am who I am today because of my loss. Squirrel is gone, but I'm here. And today, I'm telling his story and Stevie's too. Maybe the kid in the picture is trying to tell me something—that he's looking beyond me, because beyond me is where my real life is, beyond the pain. Maybe it's not such a cliché to say that Stevie and Squirrel live in me. Maybe my time remaining can make a difference, because I dared to tell my tale. Maybe Stevie and Squirrel are more than two gay park hustlers who died, but two little kids held in the promise of the cross in my hand.

I opened my hand and looked at the necklace. I stretched out the index finger of my other hand and touched the cross. Yeah. Squirrel would have wanted this. Stevie too. I put it back on. It remains around my neck to this day.

Afterword

The Crisis of Adolescence: Then and Now
By Drs. Anthony Marcus and Ric Curtis

I t is easy to imagine that the past was simpler and more whole-some; that there was a time, not so long ago, when children rode bikes and ate apples instead of devouring junk food and downloading who knows what from the Internet. Most of us assume that the world we live in now is more dangerous and complex than ever before. At the same time we sustain progressive narratives of a society that is more tolerant, open, humane, and liberal. It is this type of everyday ontology/folk wisdom that researchers need to constantly test with facts, data, and careful scholarly assessment, lest we forget that these are merely impressions and snapshots. Occasionally we are lucky enough to have something shake us from this fairy tale idea and challenge us to ask serious questions about both the past and the present. Kevin Kline's memoir of trading sex for money at the age of fourteen almost forty years ago is one of those challenges.

Kevin's memoir presents us with a very complicated and difficult past in which a fourteen-year-old boy, living in an ordinary suburb of St. Louis in 1975 with his mother and father, suddenly finds himself moving between suburban bike riding and touch football to selling sex on the streets of the inner city. He was pimped out to older and often-abusive men by an exploitative manipulator named Ray, who took advantage of his youth, naïveté, and loyalty.

Yet along the way Kevin found the type of friendship and love that he never knew was possible with two slightly older teenage boys–love that spoke to the alienation gay teens might feel in "hetero-normative" suburban homes and schools.

It seems to us that one of the key factors that drove Kevin's explorations in the summer of 1975 was the search for love, autonomy, friendship, and a world that was more true to his developing adult sensibilities than was possible in his natal family and his local high school. His first foray into this world was the chance to get a blow job and money, but as he shows us, "This is not a story about sex. This is a story about friendship and faith, about love and survival." Payment for sexual gratification may have brought him into the world of Ray the Pimp, but Stevie, Squirrel, and the chance to make his own destiny and create kinship by choice was what kept him in. He was clearly looking for something more than waiting through adolescence in silence, secrecy, and constrained choice with a family he may have loved, but did not choose. If, as most of us would agree, there is now a greater right to be sexually different, we are not sure that this alone would have resolved Kevin's crisis. For some adolescents, the right to be sexually different is crucial to their passage from childhood to adulthood, but for others, like many of the teenagers we studied, this is only a small part of their need to break out of childhood.

For his friends it was a summer of demise and eventually death. For Kevin it was the beginning of a long and painful journey to adulthood, self-discovery, and ultimately wisdom. Kevin's story compels us, the readers, to understand the stories of all those touched by teen sex trafficking, whether their experiences occurred in the past or present day.

Kevin first contacted us in 2010, after seeing a front-page article about two studies we'd done on child prostitution. Our research on what's now being called CSEC (the commercial sexual exploitation of children) and DMST (domestic minor sex trafficking) yielded several surprising findings. We discovered that the relationships between child trafficking victims and the pimps, third parties, and adult companions who helped them with their commerce were surprisingly flexible. In fact, there was a surprising absence of pimps in a population widely believed to only engage in sexual behavior through force, manipulation, and coercion. Overall, there seemed to be a remarkable amount of agency among the victims—a group, of course, with virtually no social power. Our research findings seemed to contradict much of the anti-trafficking orthodoxy that emerged as a result of the Trafficking Victims Protection Act (TVPA) of 2000.

The other, less surprising, side of it was that we found adolescents had been pitched into terrible life crises as a result of their being trafficked. This included alienation from the world of high school and family, violent customers who abused them, and exploitative police who were often the most dangerous agents in their lives. Many of the victims had become dependent on illicit, and therefore expensive, drugs. The unappealing "outer" circumstances they faced—an unlivable minimum wage, a tight formal job market, and the absence of accessible healthcare and education—further compounded their struggles. We found teenagers striving to throw off the dependencies of childhood, only to confront the narrowed choices, social sanctions, and harsh stigma reserved for those who take proscribed paths and are forced into deviant behavior.

For many of the young adults we studied, the idea that they are commercially sexually exploited children in need of protection from parents and authorities was generally taken as insulting and out of touch with their own narratives, desires, and realities. The idea that their biggest problem was trading sex for money was generally taken by the youth we studied as wrong, and obsessively focused on their sexuality—to the point of perversion. This was especially true for the majority of the sixteen- and seventeen-year-olds who work the streets. Most of these young adults had been sexually active for several years before they began trading sex for money. Some of these young people were supporting their own children and in marriage-like relationships with juridical adults who may have only been a few years older than them, but are defined by law and social service providers as criminal traffickers, by virtue of their relationships. Though a majority wanted to leave the sex trade, less than 5 percent said that they would ever seek help from social services, the law, or any other authority that so clearly denied their agency, autonomy, and personhood.

Within this world of adolescents experimenting with early adulthood, one of the things that surprised everybody, including us, the researchers, was that *almost half* of the several hundred sex-worker minors whom we interviewed and came to know in New York and Atlantic City were boys. It was this finding that put our research on the cover of newspapers across the United States in 2010 and led Kevin to contact us.

The concept of adolescence as a period of waiting and preparation for adulthood was first introduced to the United States in the pre–World War I period. Since then, it has become an increasingly mandatory identity that is now fully inscribed in law and social norms. It is no longer the voluntary choice of the most affluent 5–10 percent who, before World War I, stayed in high school until graduation. It is no longer legally, economically, ethically, or socially possible to opt out of dependence on parents. Over the past century, several of the most basic rights pertaining to citizenship and adulthood have been increasingly restricted. These include the right to: enjoy unrestricted full-time employment, drink alcohol, consent to sex, drive a car, marry without permission, buy cigarettes, serve in the military, and deny parents access to private records. In fact, "children" may now stay on their parents' medical insurance until they are twenty-six (and now thirty in some states), and are expected to submit parental tax records for financing tertiary education, into their twenties.

If adolescence is considered a period of waiting and preparation for adulthood, that preparation does not follow the nurturing path of childhood. Childhood supposes that each person has his or her own needs, and will progress according to his or her abilities. Adolescence, however, is a competitive preparation for successful adult identities. Some male teens, especially urban blacks and poor rural whites, become champion athletes to prepare themselves for the fame and fortune of their dreams. Those who are exceptionally good athletes find doors opening into highly desired jobs that have little to do with sports, but are often reserved for those with publicly demonstrated normative masculinity. Those who are ordinary athletes often settle for jobs teaching and mentoring adolescents like themselves in physical education.

For women, the drive to create a performance of femininity that mirrors the normativity of male athletes has equally powerful implications for future success in diverse careers and the marriage market. Other adolescents prepare as champion students, musicians, artists, etc., finding satisfaction in slightly more marginal, but still socially approved futures. In certain sophisticated and liberal urban environments, an adolescent may even come to be a champion homosexual these days, building dreams of the future and victories in the present around style, sexual confidence, and alternate gender performativity. For most of the boys who begin to discover the type of feelings that Kevin did in the early 1970s, we fear that they'll still be more likely to see themselves as failed heterosexuals than champion adolescent queers. The stakes of adolescent identity and performativity are, indeed, high.

For these and many other adolescents, the wait for adulthood can be unbearable because they cannot easily project a future filled with big dreams and a present filled with affirmations. For certain individuals with rough family lives, and not enough income or mental and physical space to prepare for their future, passage into adulthood can be an end in itself and the precondition for everything else. For such individuals, adulthood represents a world in which, for better or worse, they are the masters of their own destiny: they make their own friends, choose their own families, and love those with whom they are their best selves. It should be noted that such rejections of adolescence are not and probably should not be all-or-nothing affairs. We understand Kevin's journey into adulthood during that difficult summer as, unlike Stevie and Squirrel's, partial and uneven. For Kevin, it should not have been so painful to taste the joys and sorrows of adulthood, even for a summer. For Stevie and Squirrel, the experience of being pushed into adulthood was complete, destructive, and final.

In reviewing the experiences of the more than 150 boys we interviewed, we fear that the danger and destructiveness of "all or nothing" leaps from childhood into adulthood may have become worse now than in the age that Kevin describes. Adolescents under the age of eighteen who trade sex for money are no longer allowed to choose friends, colleagues, associates, companions, and lovers without the danger of sending them to prison for life. The harsh penalties directed at adults who are seen as aiding and abetting such teenagers, whether they are much older exploiters like Kevin's pimp, Ray, or more companionate and slightly older friends like Stevie (who was sixteen and would have qualified to be tried as an adult trafficker in many states) have made brief explorations even more deadly and less casual. When the stakes involve a life sentence in prison, trust is difficult, and the adults who least fear the high penalties may be the most unsafe. Authorities are viewed as inherently dangerous by all parties, and everybody is afraid to speak the truth.

Overall conditions for adolescents trying to strike out on their own into adulthood have also deteriorated significantly since 1975. The federal minimum wage (over 50 percent of minimum wage earners are under twenty-five) has dropped by roughly 30 percent in real terms. Increasingly, a college degree is needed for all but the lowliest and meanest labor. At the same time, the cost of tertiary education has risen at five times the rate of inflation. Housing prices for renters have gone up steadily as a percentage of the average hourly wage across the United States, and there are far fewer of the type of industrial/trade entry apprenticeships that used to offer an escape from poverty for emancipated late adolescents.

In particular, adolescence, a period in life that is only defined by what it is not– childhood or adulthood–has become far longer, extending further and further into the life cycle and making it more and more difficult for boys and girls to see the endpoint at which they may be fully independent and claim some control over their own destiny–sexual and otherwise.

Have things changed since 1975, when Kevin found himself in a loving street family with his friends Stevie and Squirrel, and under the dangerous influence of a manipulative pimp named Ray? The answer is clearly yes, but the challenge is in figuring out which changes are for the better, which are for the worse, and what can be done to support the difficult choices that adolescents make. We believe that there is no better place to start such an inquiry than in reading Kevin's emotionally moving, politically challenging, and socially resonant story of adolescent crisis–then and now.

–John Jay College of Criminal Justice, New York, New York

About the Authors

R. Kevin Kline is a rostered, ordained parish pastor in the ELCA (Evangelical Lutheran Church in America). Kevin has since moved from Hawaii to the mainland. He recently received approval as a mission developer and plans to foster relationships with other organizations to encourage awareness of the ongoing issues of justice in the LGBTQ community. He is a huge fan of proto-punk, the West Coast punk scene, and grunge music. He enjoys traveling and marathon running, and is a proud parent of his son, Scott. For more information on Kevin, visit www.faraway-book.com.

Daniel D. Maurer was an ELCA pastor for eleven years, serving parishes in western North Dakota. He is now a freelance writer and author of *Sobriety: A Graphic Novel*. Currently Daniel ghost-writes for a professional chef in Chicago and creates curricula for Sparkhouse, the ecumenical division of Augsburg Fortress, the official publishing house of the ELCA. He enjoys reading, writing, gardening, and playing his bagpipes. He lives with his wife and family in Saint Paul, Minnesota. For more information on Daniel, visit www.danthestoryman.com.